This series offers the concerned reader basic guidelines and *practical* applications of religion for today's world. Although decidedly Christian in focus and emphasis, the series embraces all denominations and modes of Bible-based belief relevant to our lives today. All volumes in the Steeple series are originals, freshly written to provide a fresh perspective on current—and yet timeless—human dilemmas. This is a series for our times. Among the books:

How to Read the Bible
James Fischer

Soulwinning: An Action Handbook for Christians
Reg A. Forder

A Spiritual Handbook for Women
Dandi Daley Knorr

Temptation: How Christians Can Deal with It
Frances Carroll

With God on Your Side: A Guide to Finding Self-Worth Through Total Faith
Doug Manning

A Daily Key for Today's Christians: 365 Key Texts of the New Testament
William E. Bowles

Eight Stages of Christian Growth: Human Development in Psycho-Spiritual Terms
Philip A. Captain/foreword by Jerry Falwell

How to Pray: Discovering New Spiritual Growth Through Prayer
Barbara A. Gawle

Frustration: How Christians Can Deal with It
Frances Carroll

How to Talk with God Every Day of the Year: A Book of Devotions for Twelve Positive Months
Frances Hunter

God's Conditions for Prosperity: How to Earn the Rewards of Christian Living
Charles Hunter

A Child of God: Activities for Teaching Spiritual Values to Children of All Ages
Peggy D. Jenkins

PROMISES

A Guide to Christian Commitment

Frances L. Carroll

A SPECTRUM BOOK

PRENTICE-HALL, INC., Englewood Cliffs, New Jersey 07632

Library of Congress Cataloging in Publication Data

Carroll, Frances L.
  Promises, a guide to Christian commitment.

  (Steeple books)
  "A Spectrum Book."
  Includes index.
  1. Christian life—Baptist authors.   I. Title.
II. Series.
BV4501.2.C325   1985   248.4   84-26318
ISBN 0-13-731076-5
ISBN 0-13-731068-4 (pbk.)

10 9 8 7 6 5 4 3 2 1

ISBN 0-13-731076-5

ISBN 0-13-731068-4 {PBK.}

Cover design © 1985 by Jeannette Jacobs
Manufacturing buyer: Frank Grieco

This book is available at a special discount when ordered in
bulk quantities. Contact Prentice-Hall, Inc., General
Publishing Division, Special Sales, Englewood Cliffs, N.J. 07632.

PRENTICE-HALL INTERNATIONAL (UK) LIMITED., *London*
PRENTICE-HALL OF AUSTRALIA PTY. LIMITED, *Sydney*
PRENTICE-HALL CANADA INC., *Toronto*
PRENTICE-HALL HISPANOAMERICANA, S.A., *Mexico*
PRENTICE-HALL OF INDIA PRIVATE LIMITED, *New Delhi*
PRENTICE-HALL OF JAPAN, INC., *Tokyo*
PRENTICE-HALL OF SOUTHEAST ASIA PTE. LTD., *Singapore*
WHITEHALL BOOKS LIMITED, *Wellington, New Zealand*
EDITORA PRENTICE-HALL DO BRASIL LTDA., *Rio de Janeiro*

This book is dedicated with love to:

Sydna Daily   Jane Rachel   Tom and Peggy Walker

These persons are a supportive structure through encouraging me and sharing their lives with me. Each has, in his or her own way, said, "I know Christ is at work in your life, and I am glad."

Contents

1
Believing in Christ, 1

2
The thread of commitment, 19

3
Desirable qualities of life, 35

4
God's people of commitment, 57

5
Fears, doubts, and trusting, 77

6
A commitment to grow in faith, 89

7

Learning to say "I love you," 101

8

*Considering some who have made
promises or commitments,* 115

9

Steps to take toward commitment, 129

10

Promises to cherish, 143

Index, 149

Foreword

While I was her pastor, Frances Carroll impressed me as a hard-working wife and mother, a serious Christian, and a faithful church woman. Although she is a blossoming writer, she is like many women we all know; she operates a taxi service for her children, cooks for her family, cleans the house, washes dishes and clothes, and squeezes every dollar possible out of the family budget. Besides such chores, she has her pleasures—photography, reading, fishing, camping, and rockhounding. In other words, her life is very much like yours or mine—hectic. And, through all of the hurry of her everyday life, she is trying to be Christian and grow as a Christian. So, when she writes about struggle and failure or success as a Christian, she is not pontificating from some "ivory tower." She is the neighbor next door writing out of the everyday experiences common to all of us. That is why her books are worth reading.

This book is an example of what I mean. It concentrates on personal commitment to Christ as Savior and Lord and on living in relationship to Him everyday. To put it another way, it is about making and keeping our promises to God, which we have to do in our everyday life and in spite of the ordinary obstacles of living. Keeping our promises to God is what enables us to transcend the mundane in our daily lives; it is what allows God to transform the mundane into Miracle. God is keeping His promises to us and, if we keep our promises to Him, He will turn our everyday life into "eternal life" or abundant life everyday.

Frances Carroll is her own best example of such a miracle. She has committed her life to Christ, is growing in her relationship to Him, and is keeping the promise she has made to God— to write. The result is a miracle. She still has to do the mundane chores of everyday life like the rest of us, but her life is more than mundane; it is a miracle that transcends trivia, that turns the trivial into the feeling of triumph. Life doesn't have to be mundane. It can be so much more.

Because she has experienced such a miracle in her own life, perhaps Frances Carroll can help the rest of us have a similar experience.

DR. ROY "BARNABAS" BUCKELEW
Ouchita Baptist University

Preface

"Delight yourself in the Lord; and He will give you the desires of your heart. Commit your way to the Lord, trust also in Him, and He will do it." Psalm 37: 4,5 (NAS)

Promises is a unique book for the Christian who desires more than the nominal Christian life. It allows us to understand the necessity of commitment to Christ, knowing that we, ourselves, are not capable of keeping our promises to Christ without the guidance of the Holy Spirit. *Promises* allows us to meet Christ's greatest challenge of all: "Pick up your cross and follow Me." It helps us to discover the joys of commitment to Christ in all areas of our lives and enables us to learn more about the abundant life offered to each Christian.

Commitment and promises walk hand in hand. As believers of Christ, we must become aware of our need to commit our ways to Christ and trust Him fullly. As we journey on the road of life, we will find that Christ desires to lead us into an in-depth relationship with Him. During my life, it has been my experience that most Christians aren't aware of a need to make such a commitment of faith. In fact, many Christians have yet to learn that there is more to the Christian life than what they presently understand.

Many Christians have never made a personal commitment to Christ. They have limited their walk of faith by a lack of understanding of what Christ desires each Christian life to reflect: His love. It is my hope that *Promises* will allow each reader to gain insight into the abundant life that Christ offers to each of us. To gain this insight it is necessary to make a promise of commitment to Christ.

What, then, is commitment? I think it is this: that we should seek to walk with Christ daily. That we should be receptive and willing to be called out to serve Him. That we must be willing to be more than "nominal Christians." And that we must seek the Holy Spirit to fill us with the desire to serve Christ through love and service. That we might promise to follow Christ with the insight given us every day we live and that Christ will reach out and touch our lives with His special love. Jesus Christ, our Lord and our Savior, will show us the importance of personal commitments as He directs us into a deeper relationship with Him.

As we journey on the road of life with Christ, we should be aware that we belong to Him because we have accepted the gift of grace provided on our behalf by our Savior. And with this gift there are responsibilities. Commitments to Christ aren't easy to make. We are fearful that we cannot carry through and may let Christ down. But the victories and blessings outweigh the difficulties and struggles as the Holy Spirit aids us in working through our walk of faith. We are supposed to live a life that displays the love of Christ. As we promise to be God's person, His love will flow through us, and we will learn the value of the promise of our in-depth commitment to Christ.

It is my hope that you can allow the love of Christ to flow through you, freely and unhampered, and that you will allow the promises of God to enrich your life to the fullest. Commitment to Christ in all things makes life exciting and challenging, for

He works through our lives to touch the lives of others. There is no more exciting life than the Christian lifestyle because it commits its ways to the Lord, for the Lord, Himself, moves and works through the life of the committed Christian.

Christian, take a stand and promise to serve Jesus Christ in whatever manner is pleasing to Him. With that commitment of faith then life will never be the same again. It will be filled with the blessings of the abiding life offered by Jesus Christ.

May our Lord challenge you with opportunities that will brighten your spirit and challenge you to be a person of faith and love.

Promises

1

Believing in Christ

Each step of commitment we make in our Christian lives is important but none is more important than the first step: accepting Christ's gift of salvation (eternal life). In this chapter, I would like to take a somewhat varied approach to explaining why I believe in Christ. Instead of running through a pat speech or a set plan such as the Roman Road of Salvation, I want to be more personal. Then as we approach the end of the chapter, God will lead us into insights left uncovered by my earlier thoughts.

WHY I BELIEVE IN JESUS CHRIST AS LORD AND SAVIOR

As a child, I learned of God's love for me. I expect you heard almost the same lessons and heard many of the same Bible stories that I heard as a youth. God's plan seemed good to me. I was thrilled to learn that God even sent His Son Jesus to earth so that I might know of Him.

Throughout the years the story of Jesus was told over and over again. I knew it and believed it, as most children tend to do. Jesus was real to me and I knew He had done something special to change my life. Although I did not fully understand that Jesus died for my sins and the sins of others, I knew that Jesus did something very special and I knew He did it, in part, for me. Oftentimes children don't need complicated answers to fill their hearts with Christ. Their real need and desire is to understand that Jesus' love was very real and that Jesus offers a better way of life. In my book, *How to Talk with Your Children About God,* we discuss many ideas concerning young persons. The intent of the book is to allow the young person to understand Jesus and help the child make his or her own personal commitment to Christ. I would suggest this book to anyone who desires to guide a young person to the saving knowledge of Jesus Christ. I only wish a book of this type were available when I came to Christ.

As a child, I began to understand my need for Christ. Today I realize that although my understanding of salvation (eternal life) was limited, I did believe and I did ask Jesus to come and live in my heart. When I knew I believed in Jesus, then I went forward and joined the church.

Throughout the years there were times I have wondered, "Am I really a Christian? Am I really a member of the family of God, and if I am why am I so miserable? And why don't I really grasp the full meaning of the gift of grace as offered through Christ?"

The answers to my questions did not come easily. I expect many of you have struggled over the same questions at some point in your life. Maybe even as you read my words you wonder about your salvation. If so, please read on and share my experiences. Perhaps your thoughts will be clearer at the close of this chapter.

As I sat in a Sunday School class one Sunday morning I listened as one of the men rambled on and on. He was not convinced that Christ was the chosen one sent by God to be the Savior of the world. "Where is the evidence? Other than word of mouth carried by mothers throughout the years, *there is no evidence! I doubt all of what she said and I think I have been misled into believing a fairytale,*" he stated flatly as if to deny the very existence of Christ.

Now that I look back the situation was worse than I remembered. Within the class of forty to fifty men and women, not one person spoke out in an effort to help him or speak in rebuttal. Not a single soul took out a Bible and showed him the evidence he wanted to see. That morning had a lasting impact on my Christian life. I understood that I really didn't know the facts either. In fact, I was in "spiritual poverty." I wanted to know the same things this man did and in fact what did I really believe about Christ? And what would I tell my children if they questioned me in the same manner? In an effort to learn the truth for myself, I began to search for answers. For the first time ever, I opened my Bible and read it. The answers surprised and encouraged me. Here are some of the truths I uncovered as I sought to know about Christ for myself. As I learned from the Scriptures, reading and considering the words carefully, my entire life turned from negative to positive. My family and I soon found our lives changing, and our spirits sought deeper spiritual growth. We soon moved to another church in an effort to grow and mature in our faith. Somehow, we felt, we could not receive the spiritual nourishment necessary for growth if we continued on our present course. And of course, we wanted the children to learn more about Christ and the Scriptures.

The questions I had for so many years were answered in the Scriptures. As both my husband and I studied we learned some valuable information and gained additional insight into Christ. Here is the information we learned.

I began, more or less, to study the New Testament, for Jesus' biography is located in the four gospels, Matthew, Mark, Luke, and John. The four gospels provide harmony and are written in a narrative form to provide the reader with insight concerning the life of Jesus.

I learned to study the gospels by combining the stories and picking up details concerning Christ's life and ministry. I learned that one writer gave more details than another concerning certain parts of Jesus' life and so it was necessary to read them all if I *really* wanted to know the facts.

One of the first truths I learned about Jesus' public ministry concerned John the Baptist. Recall, John the Baptist was a well-known religious figure in the community. He was well respected and had his own ministry which was of great value to God. He had been sent to prepare the way for Jesus' ministry although he did not know Jesus by name. John was an outspoken individual who bore the message, "Repent for the kingdom of heaven is at hand." Many lives were changed through John's efforts. When Christ entered the picture these people rejoiced and many became close followers of Jesus.

There were many who believed the message of John and had been baptized by John. In John 1:29–36 John introduces Jesus to the multitudes who had gathered around Him. When John saw Jesus, he immediately knew who He was. "Look! He is the Lamb of God who is to take away the world's sin. This is the One about whom I said, 'After me there is coming a man who has already been put before me, because He existed before me.' I did not know Him myself, but I came baptizing in water, that He might be made known to Israel." (verses 29–31 Williams)

Jesus was, of course, baptized by John and although I knew John had an important part in Jesus' ministry I had not realized that John called the people to recognize Jesus as the Messiah.

John pointed out the fact to two of his disciples that Jesus was the Lamb of God. When the two disciples heard Jesus speak they believed and began to follow Jesus. There was no doubt in their minds that Jesus was the "Lamb of God." These men left John's ministry to follow Christ as the first disciples.

Jesus taught many people throughout His public ministry. Jesus' early ministry is written in the gospel of John. Some of the events are:

- Jesus cleansing the temple (John 2:13–22). In this story I saw how Jesus rebuked the wrongdoers because they made His Father's house as a marketplace. He drove them out and charged them not to do this again. He wanted the temple to remain pure for the worship of God.

- Jesus foretold His death in John 2:19.

- In studying John the miracles performed by Jesus pointed to His authority as God's Son. (John 2:23–25)

- The love of Christ is displayed throughout the Gospel of John. We can read it, evaluate it, pick at it, and make our decisions about the things Jesus taught. They will stand the test. And like me, you will understand that Jesus is Savior and Lord. He cares for us deeply and has a personal commitment to each of us. His promises stand firm throughout the ages. And I am convinced that without Christ as Savior, there is no relationship with the Father.

- Jesus did not shy away from those who sought to know the truth of God. When Nicodemus met with Jesus there must have been some very lively conversation. Nicodemus was a wise man, well learned, and he was greatly affected by his visit with Jesus. Jesus spoke in a manner that assured Nicodemus that changes were necessary in his life. Jesus' spirit touched the heart of Nicodemus and moved his spirit. Contact with Jesus always leaves a lasting impression.

- Jesus' healing ministry was evidence that He had the power to cure and heal. He could change bad into good. He sat with the demonic and talked with him after He had cast out his demons. Jesus did not hurry away but took time to talk with the man and listen to his needs. Jesus took all the time the man needed to show him a better way of life through believing and trusting in Him.

- Jesus healed many others and performed many miracles during His ministry. As I read the stories of healings and miracles I knew Jesus was the Son of God and the Messiah. God's love was displayed over and over again as Christ touched lives and changed hearts. Wherever Jesus went and spirits were sensitive, lives were changed.

- As I read the Bible and recalled such events as The Sermon on the Mount (Matthew 5–7), The Tempest Stilled (Matthew 8:18–27, Mark 4:35–41), The Feeding of Five Thousand (Matthew 6:34–44, Luke 9:11–17, John 6:4–14), Jesus Walking on the Water (John 6:17, Matthew 14:23b–33, Mark 6:47–52, John 16–21), Centurions' Servant Healed (Matthew 8:1–13, Luke 7:1–10), I became well grounded in my Christian beliefs. The more I read, the more convinced I became that He was "The One sent by God."

- In reading the transfiguration episode (Matthew 17:1–13, Mark 9:2–13, Luke 9:28–36) I became convinced that Christ was not only the Savior but the Lord. The Lord impressed my mind and strengthened my heart.

It took time to read the Scriptures and seek out the truth about Christ. Yes, Jesus was and is the One Promised by God. Yes, Jesus took my sins and laid down His life on Calvary. Yes, I am forgiven and can have full fellowship with the Father because Jesus Christ, the Lamb of God, paid the price to obtain forgiveness for all sinfulness as He died, holding my sins on the cross. But best of all, Jesus did not remain in the grave, separated from life eternal, He rose from the dead. Jesus overcame the power of death and conquered Satan once and for all through the resurrection.

I Believe. The open tomb is my personal guarantee that I will live together, with Christ, in a new body, someday. Jesus sits at the right hand of God as the Holy Spirit works in my life to fulfill the promises of God. God's plan-book of life has provided everything I need through Jesus Christ and the Holy Spirit (the Helper, the Comforter, or Intercessor). God has taken care to provide for me both now and throughout eternity. God's plan for mankind was made complete through Christ.

I Believe. God raised up Christ and Christ will raise me up when He returns to earth. If I am dead and lying in my grave then *He* will claim me from the grave. My spirit will be with Him already, but the dead in Christ shall rise when Christ returns. If I live then that is all the better for I will be taken, immediately, to be with Him in the clouds. Of this there is no doubt in my mind. The Bible teaches this truth and mankind should be aware of it. God has promised it is so, and I believe it! I need not understand all the details of what God will cause to happen, and how it will happen, but merely trust God's Word and wait for God's timing to bring results. The very essence of my existence revolves around and through eternity with Christ.

I Believe. Some day, I know not when, I, like others, will stand before Christ. I will look into the face of the Wonderful One and give a full account of my life. My life will be considered and those things which were useless and empty will be burned away like wood, hay, and stubble. But at the end of the judgment, God will consider me worthy because of His Son's sacrifice and atonement for my sinfulness. I will not be disinherited, but will be welcomed into the family because Christ forgives me when I confess I have wronged. He does not hold sin over my head and bind me in guilt, He forgives completely because I belong to Him.

I Believe.   The more you know about Jesus the more you love and understand Him. You see, Jesus did not live for a select few to receive salvation but that all might come to know Him. The Bible teaches that someday every knee shall bow at the name of Jesus.

Those who will not believe, refuse to believe, or just reject Christ's gift of salvation will bow their knees as do those who believe in Christ. Their sorrow will be immeasurable, and no doubt they will wonder why they did not accept Christ as Lord and Savior. They will be eternally discouraged while we who believe will rejoice. *We have not believed in vain!* The living Lord will receive us as His own, those who are in Christ; we belong to Him for all eternity.

I Believe.   In the Holy Spirit. No one can fully explain the function and work of the Holy Spirit, but we know His work is vital to the Christian life. Our minds are limited in understanding the things that are of God, but our hearts know the Spirit is our guide. He will not fail us. The Holy Spirit can be anywhere and everywhere at once. The Holy Spirit convicts us of sin, gives new life, makes us alive in God's Word, teaches us, directs us, helps us through troubled times, and is our Comforter.

When we accept Christ as Lord and Savior, the Holy Spirit comes and lives within us. He is sent from above to perform many tasks. He is the one Christ said would show us the way to live. The Holy Spirit empowers us for Christian service, produces spiritual gifts, and gives talents. His task is an overwhelming one, in human standards, but is unlimited in the powers and understanding of the Almighty God.

The Holy Spirit teaches me that the life of Christ was the beginning point of eternity. Christ came to earth and provided a better way of life than our present sinful nature. The Spirit shows me the truth of God and allows that truth to become a functioning part of my life. The Spirit allows me to discover the person Christ desires me to be. He opens and shuts doors in my life, and yours (if you are a believer in Christ), and allows us to experience the fullness of the spirit-filled life.

The Holy Spirit will direct us in what to say, and what words to speak. He shows us that our words and actions should reflect godliness not humanness. He shows us where to place our thoughts and how to sort out good from evil. The Spirit is the one who places emphasis on Christ and directs us into deeper insight concerning God's ways. This should provide each of us with a lasting happiness unknown to those who have not made a personal commitment to Him.

The Holy Spirit continually works to fill us with the Spirit of God and supply spiritual blessings in various areas of our life. His work is valuable. Without the Holy Spirit in our lives, we might continually flounder and waver. Throughout life we might find that we have no purpose for living. The Holy Spirit is the perfect tie to the Father and the Son. He allows us to experience a part of God living within us and know happiness that without Him is unobtainable.

I Believe.   Christ is real. I believe that He is always concerned for you and me and desires all to come to Him. I believe He gives us a free choice in making decisions and living life on our own. Although He provides the information, resources, and conviction that He is the Savior of the world, He does not force us into belief. His saving gift of grace is mine because I believe in Him.

When we receive Christ as Savior every angel in heaven rejoices. But when people willingly never come to Christ as Lord and Savior, they stay eternally separated from God's fellowship. The Bible teaches this theme throughout the New Testament. God's promises are secure. When those who will not believe in Christ refuse Him eternally, they suffer a great spiritual loss.

The choice is ours! It is freely made and we are allowed many opportunities to believe in Christ and accept the gift of grace in our lifetime. The Bible tells us that we are called by God and given the Word of God. *We know there is a God,* and to refuse this moment and opportunity to believe is wrong. God does give us several chances to believe, but a time may come when there is not another chance. This is why we need to make a personal commitment to Christ now, for who knows what tomorrow will bring?

I Believe.   The evidence speaks for itself. God has made Himself clear throughout the Scriptures. I believe we are called upon to learn all we can, listen for the voice of God, and make our decisions. To make the wrong decision would be drastic, for eternal separation from the living Lord means unspeakable sorrow. In believing, accepting, and trusting the Lord, new life comes. We become adopted members of the family of God.

At this point let's read some Scriptures of importance.

JESUS IS THE LIGHT

Through our understanding that Christ sheds light in a life filled with darkness and doubt, we gain a special understanding of Him. None of us like to stand around on dark street corners or walk in a dark alley. So it is with the Christian life, we are not to live on the dark side but to seek the light, Christ's light, so we will have full confidence and trust in God.

Over and over again, the Bible teaches us we are light because the light of Christ lives within the heart of the individual Christian. It is important how your light shines before the world. And recall, your light may shine brighter than mine due to your commitment and involvement with Christ. However our lights shine, they should shine for others to see Christ in us. And the more personal Christ is to us, the deeper the light shines.

Bear in mind that it is vital for the light of Christ to shine through you and me. Christ is involved in changing lives and often He touches the life of another through us. We are His instruments of love and service. Let your light shine brightly!

- Psalms 27:1 (NAS), "The Lord is my light and my salvation; Whom shall I fear?"

- John 8:12–18 (Williams), "Then Jesus again addressed them and said, 'I am the light of the world. Whoever continues to follow me need never walk in darkness, but he will enjoy the light that means life.'
"The Pharisees then said to Him, 'You are testifying to yourself; your testimony is not true.'
"Jesus answered them, 'Even if I do testify to myself, my testimony is true, because I know where I have come from and where I am going. But you do not know where I come from or where I am going. You are judging in accordance with external standards, but I judge nobody. Even if I should judge, my decision is fair, because I am not alone, but there are two of us, I and the Father who has sent me. Even in your own law it is written, "The testimony of two persons is true," I do testify to myself, and the Father who has sent me testifies to me.' "

- John 12:35, 36 (NKJV), "Then Jesus said to them, 'A little while longer the light is with you. Walk while you have the light, lest darkness overtake you, for he who walks in darkness does not know where he is going. While you have the light, believe in the light, that you may become sons of light.' These things Jesus spoke, and departed, and was hidden from them."

- Ephesians 5:8 (NKJV), "For you were once darkness, but now you are light in the Lord. Walk as children of light."

- James 1:17, 18 (NKJV), "Every good gift and every perfect gift is from above, and comes down from the Father of lights, with whom there is no variation or shadow of turning. Of His own will

He brought us forth by the word of truth, that we might be a kind of firstfruits of His creatures."

- Revelation 21:22–27 (NKJV), "But I saw no temple in it, for the Lord God Almighty and the Lamb are its temple. And the city had no need of the sun or of the moon to shine in it, for the glory of God illuminated it, and the Lamb is its light. And the nations of those who are saved shall walk in its light, and the kings of the earth bring their glory and honor into it. Its gates shall not be shut at all by day (there shall be no night there). And they shall bring the glory and the honor of the nations into it. But there shall by no means enter it, anything that defiles, or causes an abomination, or a lie, but only those who are written in the Lamb's Book of Life."

It took some studying and talking to various ministers throughout the last few years to discover that Satan is considered spiritual darkness and Christ is light. When we look at life in a spiritual context we must consider these two forces as real, not as make-believe. Good stands firm. There are no shadows or fears in Christ, for everything is open to view. It does not hide its deeds away but displays the beauty of Christ in whatever it does.

Darkness, spiritual evil, and deception tell a different story. In darkness it is impossible to see things as they truly are. In the pitch dark of night it is practically impossible to see your hand before your eyes. Darkness hides things. Darkness, as seen reflected in evil doings and the powers of Satan, holds the hidden secrets of the night, plotting, planning, and yes, even destroying. Darkness is the unknown setting into action its plan against you while you stumble around trying to find the light.

We often stumble in the darkness and seek a better light. We want to overcome the fear of the unknown through shedding light on our spiritual problems. We do not want to be attacked in the darkness by some adversary who may steal away our spiritual happiness. Seeking the light and walking is the only security we have from fear. Christ removes fear, sinfulness, hate, and our adversaries as we walk in His perfect light.

I hope you can comprehend this example of light and dark and apply it to your spiritual life. Does Christ advise you to seek the light or to walk in the darkness concerning spiritual matters? The answer is clear. Christ wants to restore our fellowship with the Father that we might experience life to the fullest, God's way, in the light of Christ.

PAUL'S WORDS OF INSTRUCTION

Paul, the apostle, calls himself the "chief of sinners." And yet, Paul encountered Christ and made a life-changing commitment to follow the Lord. Paul's life reflects the change our lives can make from the worst possible spiritual conditions to a changed lifestyle by allowing the Holy Spirit to filter through our entire lives. The results are a usable vessel of service for the Lord. Paul's life teaches us that no matter who we are, our position in life, our sinfulness, our attitude, or our former lifestyle, Christ can and will exchange our lifestyle for something far better. It is so! He changed Paul's life and surely He wants to change ours. We can become usable vessels in service for the Living Lord serving one another in a spirit of love and happiness.

Paul's words are many and directed toward bringing us into a deeper relationship with Christ. It would be a good idea for you to use your notebook and make notes of some of the lessons you learn from Paul's commitment to Christ. Through these notes you can see the Spirit at work transforming lives. Look at what Paul teaches us:

1. "The word of the cross is to those who are perishing foolishness,

but to us who are being saved it is the power of God." 1 Corinthians 1:18 (NAS)

2. "God is faithful, through whom you were called into fellowship with His Son, Jesus Christ our Lord." 1 Corinthians 1:9 (NAS)

Okay, put up the tent, we're going to camp here for a while. Sharpen your pencil and focus your eyes on these passages. *Don't miss these words of truth.* First, the word of the cross is what? Foolishness to those who are falling away, those who will not believe. Those who will not trust Christ are perishing. They have nothing to grasp because they will not trust and believe the word of God. They walk on a "spiritual tightrope" and the line is unraveling from both ends at once. They are in a very difficult situation that will seemingly end in disaster.

Secondly, to us who are saved, it is the very power of God through the risen Savior Jesus Christ. We have to grasp the meaning of life as God has shown it through Christ. We are, indeed, a blessed people.

Thirdly, God is *faithful*. He keeps His word. He didn't change it a thousand years ago. He didn't change it today and He surely won't change it to suit our needs tomorrow. God *keeps His promises.* When God says, *I will,* you had better believe it. *He will and does keep His promises.* God hasn't allowed mankind or the forces of the adversary to alter His course one inch within the last two thousand years and surely He never will.

Fourthly, we are called into fellowship with the Father, with His Son Jesus Christ and through the Holy Spirit that lives in the family of God. No wonder we have a valid reason to rejoice over our commitments of faith and trust; we are members of God's eternal family. We can have fellowship throughout eternity with Christ.

We can look at these two verses and receive great joy for many reasons. And that is what life is all about. A deeper commitment, each day of your life and mine, will allow us to see more of God and view His preciousness with a deeper and lasting joy.

Okay, let's walk on down the path a little further and see what exciting Scriptures lie ahead. Keep your pencil handy so you can make notes on these "spiritual goodies." Don't let them escape you without understanding them and applying them to your promises made to God. Do you know that the more you read the Scriptures the happier your spirit grows? You are fed the Word of God and allowed to let it touch your spirit. It's really a blessing to know God's word and let it help you as you strive to keep your promises to the Lord.

- 1 Corinthians 2:10–16 (Williams), "For God unveiled them to us through His Spirit, for the Spirit by searching discovers everything, even the deepest truths about God. For what man can understand his own inner thoughts, except by his own spirit within him? Just so, no one but the Spirit of God can understand the thoughts of God.

  Now we have not received the spirit that belongs to the world but the Spirit that comes from God, that we may get an insight into the blessings God has graciously given us. These truths we are setting forth, not in words that man's wisdom teaches but in words that the Spirit teaches, in this way fitting spiritual words to spiritual truths.

  An unspiritual man does not accept the things that the Spirit of God teaches, for they are nonsense to him; and he cannot understand them, because they are appreciated by spiritual insight. But the spiritual man appreciates everything, and yet he himself is not really appreciated by anybody.

  For who has ever known the Lord's thoughts, so that he can instruct Him? But we now possess Christ's thoughts."

If you have ever wondered what some of the spiritual blessings are for Christians then wonder no more. Do you see what your commitment to Christ achieves within your spirit? Do you see where it makes a difference to seek the mind of Christ? Do you believe these words to be true?

What other evidence could you want concerning the life of the committed Christian? We can possess Christ's thoughts in our daily lives because we seek to know Christ. We make an effort to know Christ as more than our Savior; He is our Lord.

We could spend weeks and weeks in the Scriptures and study the truths of God. They become clearer and more practical as we seek to know and comprehend Christ's thoughts. What *blessing* and *rewards* are ours here on earth as we read our Bibles and know the very heart of the Lord.

At this point we will pull up our tent stakes and carefully pack away our spiritual tents for a while. Time is passing by ever so quickly, and there is more to learn about promises. Perhaps the greatest challenge of all is before you at this moment; press on and read the words of Paul. Read First and Second Timothy, then Colossians, Thessalonians, Philippians, and Ephesians. But don't stop there, there is more to learn and more blessings to be found as you study the Word of God and apply it to your life. Use a red or blue colored pencil and mark your Bible in the areas where the Spirit speaks to your heart. Let the word nourish your hungry soul.

Lastly, concerning my belief in Christ, let me share this thought with you. I know in whom I believe! There is no doubt that Christ is my Lord and my Savior. I have sought Him, tested Him, and proven Him. He stands the test of faith and trust, and there is no imperfection in Him. I am blessed because I belong to Him. I am grateful for God's grace issued to me through the Lamb of God. My personal goal in life is to serve Him and allow His love to flow through my veins. I have made a personal promise to live my life for Him. It is my hope that you are involved in a similar promise to serve as a vessel of love and promise to all you meet in the name of Christ. Press on, faithful friend in

Christ. There is much to learn so that we can use our spiritual tools and gifts for the Lord in building part of the Kingdom.

You may wish to use a notebook to record the answers to the end-of-chapter questions. Be honest about your answers. It is important that you realize your true feelings concerning Christ.

Questions

1. Do you believe in Christ as your Lord and Savior?

2. What evidence do you have that your faith is real?

3. Is a personal commitment to Christ necessary if you desire to follow Him? Why is this so?

4. Consider four things Christ did here on earth that you consider important. List them in your notebook and give the reasons why you consider them to be important.

5. Which, in your opinion, do you believe would have been easier:(A) To believe in and follow Jesus in the times described in the Bible, (B) To believe in Christ today now that we have the Bible, (C) To believe when we find the time convenient and we are through "kicking up our heels"? Give several reasons for your answer to this question.

6. Why did God provide everything we needed through Christ and the Holy Spirit?

2

The thread of commitment

The thread of commitment weaves its way throughout the Christian life. The design formed depends largely upon our involvement in the Christian life and our willingness to respond to Christ's call to "Take up your cross and follow Me."

When our commitment of faith is nominal, the pattern woven in the fabric of life may cause only a tinge of change, allowing the threads to alter the design of our lives ever so slightly. Little or no change has come because we have not dared to make a full commitment to Christ as leader of our lives. But with deeper commitment the threads give harmony and lend color to life. Our Christian lives can and should become a kaleidoscope of color showing the patterns formed as rainbows of promise and peacefulness. At any moment in our lives other people should see a rainbow reflection bringing gladness and calmness to the troubled waters of life. Our lives are a mirror image of our belief and commitment to the living Lord.

The pattern woven throughout our lives reveals the truth concerning our faith. When the threads of commitment disperse into the fabric of life, the facts are self-evident. We grasp the visible fact that our personal commitments are often shallow and fade away with the passing of time. And we become convinced that we do not fully understand God's blueprint for our lives.

You see, God's powers and promises to those who love Him are limitless. We who believe in Christ belong to God. The more spiritual insight we gain and the more we learn from reading the Scriptures, the more involved we become in God's plan for the Christian life. As our convictions grow deeper, our commitment of faith and trust in Christ develops and expands. This allows us to reach new horizons in our walk of faith. As we allow ourselves the privilege of understanding God's power, our faith will be proven and verified as genuine and solid. No longer will we be prone to wonder, for our wisdom has guided us into a deeper insight concerning the Lord.

Let's look at some verses of Scripture that lend strength to this idea. Studying Scriptures as a resource guide of God's truth allows us to understand the promises of God to His people. God's pledges are trustworthy and not given lightly. Through our understanding of God's unwavering love and concern we will stand ready to make a deeper and more meaningful profession of faith. As we acknowledge God's involvement with Christian believers we should be greatly humbled. Just look at some of God's words as written in the Bible.

- Acts 16:31b (NKJV), "Believe in the Lord Jesus Christ, and you will be saved."

- John 6:46–48 (NKJV), "Not that anyone has seen the Father, except He who is from God; He has seen the Father. Most assuredly, I say to you, he who believes in Me has everlasting life. I am the bread of life."

- John 10:27–30 (NKJV), "My sheep hear My voice, and I know them, and they follow Me. And I give them eternal life, and they shall never perish; neither shall anyone snatch them out of My hand. My Father, who has given them to Me, is greater than all; and no one is able to snatch them out of My Father's hand. I and My Father are one."

- 1 John 2:3, 5 (NKJV), "Now by this we know that we know Him, if we keep His commandments . . . But whoever keeps His word, truly the love of God is perfected in him. By this we know that we are in Him."

- 1 John 3:1–3 (NKJV), "Behold what manner of love the Father has bestowed on us, that we should be called children of God! Therefore the world does not know us, because it did not know Him. Beloved, now we are children of God; and it has not yet been revealed what we shall be, but we know that when He is revealed, we shall be like Him, for we shall see Him as He is."

- Psalm 34:22 (NAS), "The Lord redeems the soul of His servants; and none of those who take refuge in Him will be condemned."

- Hebrews 6:9, 10 (NAS), ". . . Beloved, we are convinced of better things concerning you, and things that accompany salvation, though we are speaking in this way. For God is not unjust so as to forget your work and the love which you have shown toward His name, in having ministered and in still ministering to the saints."

What words of comfort and encouragement! The Christian heart should feel inexpressible joy as we ponder these thoughts. Contemplate these thoughts concerning the verses above:

- When we believe Christ died for our sins and accept His perfect gift of grace, we are changed in spirit and in nature. We become new spirits living within the same body but now our spirit turns toward God and away from evil. We no longer seek the things that divide us from God but look for the things that will draw us nearer to Him. Sin, separation from God's holiness and His love, cause us to wilt and fade away (in the spiritual sense). But Christ has given us new lives and saved us from the horror of an eternal hell. We receive eternal security and everlasting life because Christ laid down His beautiful life for our ugly sinfulness.

- Christ is our personal shepherd. He tends us, He cares for us, He is *everything we need*. Throughout the storms of life when we feel empty and alone our shepherd is near. He has not left us to wander aimlessly into harm or to fall into circumstances for which there is no way out. Christ, our gentle shepherd, has given His word; He has not left us without help or hope.

- When we keep His word the love of God is perfected within us. No flaws, no imperfections, not even a blemish; perfect love.

- We are called children of God because we have accepted Christ's gift of atonement. We believe; we desire to follow goodness and mercy and set aside evil and wickedness. As adopted children of God we have many promises hidden away for us.

- When He is revealed, we shall be like Him and see Him as He is. How is He? He is complete, lacking in nothing, perfect, pure, completely godly.

These are but a few of the words of encouragement provided for us throughout the Bible. These words enlighten and uplift us as we find new hope in our studies. We should recall that gifts given by God are given freely. We can not do anything good enough or merit enough reward to consider our rewards as more than a gift. We merely accept them and thank God for them. With the acceptance of God's promises we will desire more than nominal Christianity. We will desire to honor Christ by altering the unlovely, the ugly, the deceitful conditions which prevail in our lives. The desire to pledge our lives to Christ and seek God's ways should become an all important goal in our walk with Christ.

I can almost hear you ask, "How do I begin to change my lifestyle? Can I truly learn to be a Christ-centered person? Is the goal of a deeper commitment to Christ feasible?" These questions are easily answered and we can make short work of our response. Christ has left nothing to chance in the Christian life. And when we begin to respond to Christ one step at a time we become more sensitive to Christ's call. His Spirit is a willing teacher that lives in each believer. He has taken the Christians from the lion's den and removed the stumbling blocks in the road of life. Our chief need, as believers, is in understanding that there is more to the

Christian life than most of us realize, and few of us are seeking the abundant life that Christ has to offer.

Through an open commitment to Christ we say yes to God. Yes, Lord, it is my desire for You to show me the person You want me to be. I desire to work in Your fields and plans the seeds of love, joy, kindness, peace, happiness, and concern. With a genuine commitment to Christ there is an unshakable knowledge and understanding that God's promises never waver.

Let's look at some of the various commitments we tend to make.

PROJECTS

We often make commitments to work on various projects of interest to us. Perhaps it is a P.T.A. project conducted at your child's school. You promise to help. You work hard, along with many others, to achieve success. You went all out in your efforts and the P.T.A. was able to achieve its goal by providing the money for P.T.A. activities. You are glad that you were able to contribute some of your time, talents, and efforts to achieving a goal.

You see, your time and talents are important, your promises were kept, and the results were good. The commitment to task was fun and rewarding.

IDEAS

We make a commitment to an idea. I'll bet you've seen them, I know I have, persons so consumed with an idea or a plan that nothing else seemed worthwhile. Seeing an idea through from start to finish because it achieves an all important personal goal is not all that unusual. As results are seen and approved of, by you, the plan becomes a reality. Weren't you glad for the time you spent, the effort you made, and the promise you made to see this thing through? Of course you were.

Our ideas and goals make the achieving of goals an important part of life. Ideas make a difference in our Christian lives too and as we share our ideas with others results will be seen. We should never overlook our potential in exploring ideas and goals within the body of believers. We have only begun to achieve the goals and see the results of Christ working among us. As we promise to do our part, share our plans and ideas, Christ works among us to unite our spirits in love and grace.

COMMITMENT TO A JOB AND A CAREER

Commitment to obtain a job you desire is not unusual. A better job makes us feel that success is within our reach. A better job may mean a better way of life or the obtaining of some things which were unobtainable before. Almost all of us want to get ahead and oftentimes that opportunity comes through working. Sometimes it is within our power to claim the things we want but more often than not we find ourselves hoping for the best. There are many people who set goals for themselves to claim a certain position within a company only to find that when it is theirs they are still not content.

Thousands upon thousands of us toil and sweat trying to find happiness. It might surprise you to know that jobs very seldom bring permanent happiness. Happiness is found in attitudes of the heart and not in the things we possess.

COMMITMENTS TO OUR FAMILY

Commitments to our family. Who among us doesn't want the best for our children? None of us wants our children to do without the very basics of life. None of us looks forward to struggles within our family. We want our lives to be full and happy. We want to be content in life. We want to do whatever we can to make life better for our loved ones. The balance between needs and luxuries often overlaps. As parents, one of our greatest struggles is to maintain a proper balance and not give in to unnecessary whims and desires which will give our children more than they really need. Our love need not be paid out to children in things, but given as immeasurable gifts of love, faith, a firm foundation to build their lives upon, and true self-esteem. These are the important things in life.

You see, our commitment to the family is to provide a well-balanced spiritual, physical, and material life. An imbalance of one or more of these elements may cause our young people a great deal of unhappiness and trouble. The things which really matter are not measured in the hand or seen with the eye, but felt within the heart.

PARENTS

Commitment to parents. We must not forget our parents and the loving relationship we have with them. These threads of commitment should not become tangled or broken as our parents age. Although we have other commitments and a different lifestyle, there is no excuse for unwise consideration of our parents and their needs. Their need for love has not lessened within the years and in their declining years there is a desire to be near the ones they love the most. Let the thread of commitment run true and straight as we reach out and touch their lives. More than likely your parents, as did mine, made countless sacrifices for you. They did what they could to provide you with a good beginning. It might even be wise for us to consider the moments of illness we encountered as children, the needs we had for clothes, books, all those things a child needs that we consider all important.

Our parents did their best to meet those needs. Now are we meeting theirs?

In days gone by children assumed responsibility for their parents in their later years. I recall my grandfather living with us when I was just a tiny little girl. "Papa Grand" had a room of his own, in our house, and he was a part of the family. He lived with mother and daddy until the day he died. My parents, like many others, took care of the needs of their elders. But today things are almost in reverse.

Many of us tend to "push" our parents on some other member of the family or "place them in a home." I am deeply concerned that this attitude has allowed us the freedom to avoid our responsibilities. While I am sure that some older people need the security and care of a nursing home or a retirement village, let us consider their emotional needs equally. Do they really want to be in a home or retirement village? If they do then things are fine, but what if they want something else? Surely, you and I would not want to be pushed off onto someone or sent somewhere we didn't want to go. As long as an older person is responsible, mentally, and physically alert than they have a full life to live. The love offered by a grandparent or parent is without measure. Lucky is the person who can touch lives with their elders.

I would be glad to touch lives with my mother or my grandparents if they were alive today. But now that they have died there is a void. It would be nice to have a granddaddy who could tell me of days gone by and how it was when he was a boy. Consider the offerings of love, wisdom, and happiness that an older person can lend to your life. Allow them to tell you stories and recall the old days, for sometime, when you least expect it, they will be gone. You will be left with a very empty place that needs to be filled with the loving wisdom and kindness of an older person. We are more responsible for our parents than most of us are willing to admit. Don't overlook your need to respond to your parent in Christ-like love. You'll be glad you did. And you know, Christian friend, our parents' lives are as important as any other life we touch in the name of Christ. Jesus provided for His mother, Mary, in His last moments; can we do any less for our parents?

Even the older person who is limited because of age and health has special needs. It is disobedience to God's commands if we ignore our parents and turn away from them because we want to do something else or have a different lifestyle. When there are special reasons for parents to be treated in a different manner then we should carefully weigh our thoughts and motives. If we find we ignore and reject older people because we don't want to be around them, that attitude is totally wrong, and we had better know that God does not view this attitude as an honorable one. The Scriptures teach us to honor our father and mother that our days might be long.

Recall your past. If there were events and happenings which caused problems or hurt you then you need to forgive and try to forget. Allow your spirit to be freed from past mistakes. Perhaps your parents, like mine, didn't do everything right and you felt life was unfair. Well, if this is true then know this, at least they tried. They made mistakes and tried to do what was right and proper for you, in their eyes. Only God knows their success or failure.

I have learned being a parent isn't easy, and it's hard to know what to do. Perhaps the mistakes I made with my children can be forgiven and forgotten and my children will someday judge me as a mother who really tried to do right. I have often wondered if we are making the right decisions when we encourage, discipline, and love our children in a given situation. But whatever happens, I know, as does God, that we have tried to be fair.

THICK AND THIN

Commitments to go on through thick and thin. Sometimes it isn't easy to continue on the road of life when the road gets bumpy and we have no map. There are moments when each of us feels like giving up. But somehow we continue on. The feeling that things are going to get better gives us living hope.

Sometimes I feel that the thick and thin of life has gotten too thick. It seems that things cannot get any worse than they are, yet we have hope. Were it not for our commitment to the living Lord and our knowledge that Christ can overcome any circumstance, there would be no hope.

In a day in which life seems tossed around like a beachball at a seaside resort, many of us ignore making a commitment to live for Christ. We skip around from one thing to another and cannot find peace within because we are not willing to step forward and live the Christian lifestyle as God intended it to be. How sad! Too many people are under duress, imprisoned by mental attitudes of inadequacy because they are unwilling to live according to their beliefs. Instead, many lash out and try to fight their way through the forces of darkness and doubt, while others meekly give in and allow topsy-turvy patterns to dominate their lifestyle. Ours is to cultivate the positive aspects of our faith and set aside unhealthy attitudes. The life of the believer should reflect positive action and set aside negative forces as they arise.

PERSONAL COMMITMENTS

Personal commitments to one another. One of the weakest areas we all encounter is the vulnerable link in the chain of commitment to one another. Recall how our forefathers lived their lives. Their name and their reputation was just about all most of them had. A man or woman's word of honor was a bond of commitment and promise that few reneged on. When a person said they would do something, it was done completely and with little, if any, consideration of going back on their word. With the promise made there was an all out effort to "do their best" to prove themselves as persons of honor. Consider how lightly the word *promise* is often used today. We toss around promises like a rubberball and seldom consider the impact of the broken promise on the life of another.

We seem unimpressed by the person who promises to do something, gives his or her word, and carries through with personal commitment. Because we have become a vulnerable society we no longer consider personal promises necessary. Few people make strong promises anymore because we might decide we really don't want to keep our promises at all. Time and time again we look for a way to back out of a situation and fail the test of honor. Half-finished or barely developed plans cause us to bungle our promises and cause us to perform our task half-heartedly. Many of us never make a commitment to anyone because we do not want another to see we have an Achilles' heel and think we are weak. The truth is that keeping our promises makes us stronger.

But the fact still remains that we who believe and trust in Christ must determine the need for personal commitments to Him. We have to set a standard. And when we fall short or do a so-so job then we must face up to the truth that we are not perfect. We may have done our best, fallen on our faces, blemished another's view of us, but at least we were trying. The challenge is to step forward and try, and Christ will provide the victories at the opportune moment.

Only through commitment of our lives will we achieve something lasting. And after all, very few people really cast stones at those of us who make serious commitments to our faith. There are only a handful of troublemakers, gossips, idlers, and those wrongly influenced by others who dare to continually try and crush our spirits and eliminate our Christian faith. And after all is said and done they are but a song in the wind and will last but a moment. For the person who knows the importance of touching lives will press on no matter what others say or do. The person who never steps out and makes a commitment to another has allowed some of their joy to be stolen away from them. Only as we touch lives and share with others will they learn the importance of the Christian's commitment to life.

FAITH

Commitment to share our faith. Have you allowed the Lord Jesus Christ to fill your spirit with His loving nature? Is Christ a personal Savior to you? Are you moved spiritually when you consider Christ's gift to those who will believe? Is your faith in Christ sure enough that you feel a need to share it? What obligations do you have in sharing your faith? These are but a few of the questions you and I must ponder concerning our faith. Later on we will answer these questions one by one. But for now we must know this, Christian friend; we who believe in Christ are a part of the family of God. We have been called to a different way of life. A better, more holy way of life. With that calling and the answering of the call we are answerable to Christ in the sharing of our faith. We will want our light to shine forth so that others may experience the completeness of life that Christ intends all to have.

The sharing of our faith takes a personal involvement of our lives with the lives of others. The Christian experience is a personal walk with a personal Lord and Savior. While we share common experiences with other Christians, each Christian is an individual and has individual needs. As we share our faith and how the Lord has guided us through the darkness and brought us into the Light (His Light), we will find that other persons experience some of the same problems and heartaches we have had. If there is any one thing I have learned through writing, it is that many of you have faced and endured problems and struggles similar to mine.

By sharing my faith on these pages other persons are able to deal with their own heartaches and difficulties. One young woman said, "I thought I was an isolated case and that nobody ever had problems like mine. When I read *A Book of Devotions for Today's Woman,* I was overjoyed. You laid your life open for everyone to see, and many of your struggles were the same struggles I have now." This young woman found help for her problems through this book and now she is learning to face life anew. Christ shows us how to share our faith when the timing is right. What one person needs to hear concerning the Christian way of life may not be the same ideas another person needs expressed to them. We will want to let the Lord show us when and how to speak, and to whom.

Our walk of life concentrates on Christ in our lives. The closer we are to Christ, the more evidence of our trust and faith in Him shows. We need to develop a closer bond with Christ so that our faith will become practical and usable. As we claim the promises of the Christ we will feel a call to walk in a more Christ-like manner. We will allow our faith to display God's total grace among us. Our faith will show through in even the most adverse of circumstances. And the more our faith functions the nearer we will draw to our Redeemer. Faith is in continual action. It is drawn on moment by moment and allows Christ to work freely within the life of the believer.

PROMISES MADE, PROMISES KEPT

Within our lives there are many opportunities to make numerous promises. The promises spoken with our lips are verbal pledges to another. With each promise there is an obligation to carry through and see that our word is kept.

Consider others as more important than yourself. Shoulder part of someone else's burdens and watch how your life will be enriched. You see, dear friend, it is through caring and sharing of yourself, unselfishly, that life gathers some of its earthly rewards. Soon you will find yourself involved with bearing a part of other's burdens not because you have to, but because you want to.

COMMITMENT TO PRAY

Our Lord wants us to make a commitment to pray. You may not be called upon to pray for an individual on a daily basis but then again you might. Many a loving mother has prayed for her son or daughter to come to know Christ or that their children would find a deeper understanding of the Christian life.

One woman approached me after a recent speaking engagement, "Your words are true about praying and planting seeds of faith as we pray for our children. Only God and I know how I have prayed for a certain matter concerning my son. I have prayed for more than fifteen years for my son. He has been in my prayers throughout the day and well into each night. I asked the Lord to lead my son into the light of truth. My prayer was answered last week," she said with a tear trickling down her cheek. Her smile of loving faith told me that a son was very blessed to have a mother like the one that stood before me.

Commitments to pray should never be taken lightly or assumed with a careless attitude. The prayer warrior is one who is ready to stand before the Lord and pray, with faith, trusting the Lord God to answer in His way. The prayer warrior is involved in life and is willing to make a commitment to prayer and wait for results. None of us can ever know the effect we have on the life of another, especially where prayer is concerned. The prayer of the child of God is all important. Never underestimate God's work in your life as you pray.

There are various commitments to be made within a lifetime. The scarlet thread of commitment should run straight and true in the Christian life. As we walk through life let us journey so that our threads of promise and commitment will run true and not cause the pattern of life to weave to and fro. We are to walk a straight path and commit our ways to the living Lord.

Questions

1. Why are promises an important part of the Christian life?
2. What are some commitments we make in our lives?
3. Why do some people hesitate in making promises?
4. Locate three promises in the Scriptures which bring comfort and happiness to your spirit.
5. Why is it important for you to know some of the promises contained in the Scriptures?
6. Have you made a commitment of faith to Jesus Christ as your personal Lord and Savior?
7. Consider life without a commitment to Christ. Now consider the life of the Christian who promises to be Christ's person. In your notebook create the following headings: "Without Christ" and "With Christ." List the difference in the two lifestyles.
8. Why do we avoid involvement in helping others by sharing their needs and burdens?
9. How do Christians realize joy and victory in their lives?
10. Consider the thread of commitment as it runs through the fabric of your life. Write a brief description of the pattern it weaves throughout your life.
11. Are there some areas of your life where you have neglected commitments to Christ and others in your life? When and why?
12. Are you willing to become more receptive to God's call for you to be His person?
13. Paul, the apostle, said, "Show yourself an example of those who believe." Consider this idea. What do others see that reflects the love of Christ within you?

3
Desirable qualities of life

As we have seen, commitment is not an easy thing to achieve. It takes effort to become aware of the needs and burdens around us. In this chapter we will determine some of the desirable qualities of life. By looking at the desirable qualities of life we will focus in on the positive areas of life, setting the negative in its proper place, away from the Christ-centered walk of life.

THE PURPOSE OF COMMITMENT IN OUR LIVES

Have you wondered why Christ did not turn aside His commitments to God and do something other than God's will? Now be honest about it—haven't you? I know there have been moments in my life when I have turned aside my commitments and run away to avoid facing up to situations. But Christ didn't do that! When I consider why Christ did not run away or alter the situations He found Himself in, in those last days before His death, *it overwhelms me.*

Jesus prayed three times to His Father, God, and asked if there were another way that God might achieve His plan for mankind. We know that Jesus also prayed stating the truth that if there were no better way then He was willing to pay the price. He was willing to submit His life for the payment of our sinfulness. Christ, being a member of the Trinity, could have removed Himself from this situation at any moment but He did not. He chose to follow through on God's plan and meet His commitment. His commitment to God's plan of eternal grace was fulfilled. The results gave us a choice concerning spiritual renewal, new life through Christ, or spiritual death and separation from God. The choice is ours and we make it freely and willingly.

It took an all out effort for Jesus Christ, the man, to carry through on His commitment to God. Never think, for one moment, that Christ did not suffer mental, spiritual, and physical anguish in His last days. Although He knew that God's blueprint for mankind was to be completed through His sacrifice, Christ still experienced heartache and struggles. It was not an easy course to follow, but He did. Consider what would have happened to you and me if Jesus Christ had changed His mind and run away from His commitments. Christ's life is the perfect example of the ultimate commitment to God. Ours is to grow and mature in spirit so we can say, "It is not I who is important but Christ living within me." With this attitude our spirits can begin to receive a regenerated spirit of love and happiness for true life is found in Christ not within ourselves.

The purpose of commitment in our lives is this: to draw us nearer to the Father. For without a promise to follow after Christ and walk as He walked, our lives are shallow and empty. Love isn't love until commitment is made. Christ is perfect love offered to you and me. With our loving commitment to Christ, God-like love begins to flow through our spiritual hearts. When we make a promise to draw closer to Christ new opportunities arise to serve Christ. Life has grown more precious as we begin to be

Christ's person and accept the greatest challenge of all, following Christ's spiritual blueprint for life. In fact our lives begin to focus in on the important things concerning life and the trivial matters are viewed as unimportant. Our walk of faith today determines our usefulness in the sharing of our beliefs. It is difficult to share something you have no knowledge of and so it is with commitment. If you never made a full commitment to Christ then you cannot possibly know what it is all about. Your mirror image of commitment allows you to gain a little insight into involvement on a deeper level, but still the shadows keep you from seeing the clear image. Christ wants you to realize there is more than you see, and when you make a personal commitment to Him the image will grow brighter. Not all Christians view life from the same angle. The deeper the commitment the more understanding Christ gives us concerning the secrets of life.

THE CHALLENGE OF COMMITMENT

For persons seeking unusual challenges in their lives here is the greatest challenge of all—dedicate your life, as it is, as it will become, and as it takes on deeper meaning, 100 percent to serving Jesus Christ. Do this and notice the things that will begin to happen. There is no greater commitment of lifestyle, faith, and trust than this. Truthfully, few of us seem willing to accept the challenge, thus robbing our lives of many blessings in serving others in a Christ-like manner.

The challenge is a bold one. It is one that requires discipline of mind, spirit, and habits. It is one that says, "Christ is first in my life." The Christ-like commitment is one that is in continual training and is always learning. It is a life that reaches for a new tomorrow while sharing your faith today.

The challenge of commitment runs deeper than any commitment any champion athlete ever made, for it involves a lifelong commitment not to self or self-achievement but to Jesus Christ. Sounds frightening doesn't it? Well, it need not be for as we begin to understand the need for a personal commitment of faith then we become aware of a better way of life, Christ's way. Often we become attuned to the fact that what we have going in our lives now isn't all that great, and a change for the better is found by dedication to Christ our Lord.

I realize that the challenge is not suitable for everyone. Most Christians ignore the challenge of commitment only to find that their lifetime walk with Christ is missing an important ingredient. That ingredient is full fellowship with the Lord. For as we walk with Christ our lifestyle is determined not in materialistic values and goals but in achieving a close relationship with God. When we consider the blessings of commitment and the reward of understanding the deeper things of God this should outweigh our fears and lack of confidence. We will never know what spiritual blessings are ours until we seek them. We will only know we have missed something and not lay hold of it because we neglected a personal commitment to God.

The challenge of commitment is to seek and lay hold of the riches of God laid away for each believer. These blessings include such things as:

- A one to one relationship with the living Lord
- Deeper understanding of the days ahead and eternity
- Unshakable security in Christ
- Peace of mind and spirit in every situation
- A deeper spiritual life
- Opportunities to serve in the household of faith
- Challenges which result in unspeakable joy
- Knowledge of Christ's gift of salvation at a deeper level
- Spiritual riches that are irrevocable
- Insights and wisdom, gifts from the Spirit

The opportunity to sow or water seeds of faith

- A fullness of life that is unrealized and unaccepted in the nominal Christian life

- Having Christ use your life in a manner which will glorify Him

- A wisdom that allows you to understand that eternity is more than being with Christ forever. It is a wisdom that teaches you that the things you do now are important in helping others find a deeper fellowship with Christ.

- The blessings of knowing and seeing Christ allow you to be a functioning part of the body of Christ, the church, and allow you to refresh, renew, and restore some weakness within the body through the power of the Holy Spirit that lives within you.

There are numerous rewards that are ours through a personal commitment to Christ Jesus. Many of them must be learned on your own and for me to speak of them at this point is not to be. For you see, many of us are simply not prepared to accept the gifts and blessings of the deeper life and shy away when we consider that all these rewards and blessings are ours as gifts from the Lord through our commitment to total faith and trust in Him. In the beginning of commitment there are many questions which come to mind:

1. How can I ever be all Christ wants me to be?
2. Why has God chosen me for this task?
3. How can I do the things Christ wants me to do when I feel so inadequate?
4. Why are others waiting for me to act as a guide in these troubled times?

Instead of putting these questions to rest and allowing the Spirit to answer them, we find ourselves wrestling with them. I know how difficult it is for you to believe that Christ has a plan for you. I've been there. And it is almost impossible to humanly reason through the "whys" and "hows" of commitment. The answers are found in accepting the challenges provided by Christ with a humbled spirit and gladness of heart. Ours is to say, "Yes, Lord Jesus Christ, I want to accept the challenges you have for me. Lord, although I'm unsure and uncertain of my abilities and talents, I know you can achieve anything you want through me. I'm yours Lord, heart, soul, and spirit. I'm ready for the deeper life and the richer life you have stored up for me. I am your vessel, your tool, and your instrument of love and service."

There is no greater challenge than taking the step of total commitment to Christ. For now that you believe and accept the gift of salvation you understand there is a closer relationship with the Savior available for those who are daring enough to accept the quiet call of the Holy Spirit, "Be mine all the time and allow Me to work through your life to show others Christ."

THE CHRIST-CENTERED PERSON

You've seen them somewhere, sometime, within the last few years. They are everywhere, you know, and something about them makes them stand out in a crowd of other Christians. Perhaps their faces appear to radiate a glow of happiness and peace as you look into their eyes. Or, maybe, their attitudes seem different from others. Whatever it is or wherever you see him or her there is no doubt that this person is different. This is the Christ-centered person.

One of the interesting things about Christ-centered people is this; we are either repelled by a force which moves us away from them or we are drawn to their godliness. The Christ-centered person need not say a word or make a movement for us to become aware of a powerful commitment to Christ. He or she is different, so different, that to the spiritual values within us a silent alarm goes off and says, "Hey, look at this person, he's special. Or, she's got that something that you secretly want." And you find yourself wondering how this unique person obtained that secret ingredient in life that sets one apart from the crowd. Such Christians stand out wherever they are and perhaps they never know they radiate that loving glow.

Recently I spoke at a gathering of women. I am basically a very shy and quiet person until you know me and I know you. As I sat in the room talking with the women I noticed one woman on the other side of the room. She had positioned herself as far away from the rest of the group as she could. She sat on a kitchen stool and listened quietly for a long while. The conversation revolved around my life as a writer, why I wrote, how I wrote, and where I got my ideas.

I felt at ease as I spoke with these women. Although it is difficult for me to concentrate on myself and share myself with others, Christ is teaching me the importance of His gifts to me as I write and share my books with others. The women were happy when I said, "I've just begun writing my sixth book." When someone asked what the subject matter would be I swallowed hard and replied, "Promises and commitment to Christ in our daily lives."

One woman responded that this was a good subject. Another woman said she knew she needed to make a commitment to Christ, so on and so on. The woman at the other end of the room spoke up, "Can I say something?" she asked. "Sure, anything you want," I said.

"Did you know you radiate a certain glow about you when you talk about what you are doing? Your entire personality bubbles and glows as you talk about what Christ is doing in your life," she said in a matter-of-fact tone.

"Well, thank you," I said. "I'm happy doing the things I am doing now and for the first time in my life, I know real happiness and joy."

Someone replied, "That's apparent because I've never seen a look on anyone's face like I see on yours right now." I was surprised by the response of these women as I spoke to them. "Can we ask you anything we want to?" one person asked.

"Sure, I guess so. If I don't know the answer or am unsure about how to answer I may not reply to the question though," I said with a smile. For over two hours they asked me questions and I answered. We were communicating not as a group but as individuals concerned with our lives and the lives of others. It was a wonderful time of sharing and understanding. Time and time again someone would say, "I've always wanted to ask this but didn't know whom to ask. . . ." or "What do you think about this?" or "Somebody says we have to do this, or that, and if we don't then we really aren't children of God. Is this true?"

All through the evening we questioned, discussed, and reasoned through the truths of God and the standards of mankind. It was a wonderful evening and the presence of the Holy Spirit filled the air as we spoke in loving truth about the needs of the church, our families, our community, and of certain individuals. One woman said, "Why have I never talked with you before? I've seen you at least one hundred times and barely spoken to you at all?" I assured her that I really didn't have all the answers and was no expert on many areas of life and she said, "But you are, don't you see that you are really reaffirming the beliefs of almost every person here? God sent you here to give us a boost and let us know that our spirits need to test the words we hear and know what is true and what is not. We are testing you, tonight, here and now, and your words are not misleading us. You are being led by God."

The challenge of that night has not been quickly forgotten. Not because I radiate and glow but because I see the needs other people have in a different light than before. Their need is like mine, to know the Word (and they do), to be sure that the one who teaches, preaches, or instructs is accurate and not twisting the Word of God, and to determine what course to take as God shares His Word with each individual. That night found a group of committed Christian women encouraged and uplifted because they had not swayed with the tide of current trends but having stood firm in Christ they were prepared to press on and renew their personal promises to Christ.

My challenge in that speaking engagement was not in proving myself but in making sure that I spoke with God's guidance and not as I thought would bring results. I found myself listening to each question fully and responding not in attitudes of my natural heart but in the Spirit of the living Lord. It was an exhausting evening for me and as I drove home my heart was very happy to have met with these women. I thought, "What greater challenge do you have in store for me, Lord? Why was it important for me to be questioned so severely and so thoroughly tonight?" I even wondered if I had measured up to God's standards as I sought to give the right answer. That night as I tried to sleep God filled my heart with these words:

"My precious child, my daughter, you have done well. I promised you that as you sought to be my woman, a Spirit-filled woman, I would give you opportunities. You have only just begun to serve Me.

"Keep yourself in the Word of God. Be sensitive to my speaking, my calling, in your life. Consider not the ways of the world but the challenges of Christ in you. When you do these things, as you have tonight, I will use you as a vessel of love and concern for all people. Seek not your own personal self-gratification nor a super high spiritual experience for those are meaningless and temporary experiences but seek Christ only. I AM the meaning to life and give life. It is through Me that you find life and not through your own words and thoughts. I want to use you as an instrument of love and sharing and I will do so as you remain sensitive to Me and those in my charge. Seek the things above and set your mind toward Christ. Press on, faithful child."

The challenge, the call to the committed life are for all, not for a select few. Each one of us is called to shed their own light in the dark corners of the world. While you, like myself, might not consider yourself a glowing personality we must be aware that we do share the light of Christ in our own special and unique manner. Ours is to lighten the load of another so that they might better see the love of Christ as it shines through. What greater challenge could you or I ask for than this?

VIEWING THE CHRIST-LED PERSON

What makes the Christ-led person different in the eyes of the world than the ordinary person? *Everything!*

1. A continual devotion to God.
2. Priorities set and straight.
3. A certain spirit about him or her.
4. A sure fellowship with the Spirit of Christ.
5. Willingness to be flexible.
6. Approachable concerning the needs of others.
7. Less of a talker and more of a listener.
8. Lives with the love of God in one's heart.
9. Sensitive to the point of being earthly vulnerable.
10. Avoids ungodly chatter and gossip.
11. Life is yielded not to selfishness but to Godliness.
12. An effective testimony of Christ in daily life.
13. Less concerned with popular opinion and more concerned about Christ's opinion.

14. Open communication with the loving Father.

15. Responds to life and does not neglect to provide God the opportunity to use oneself as a vessel of communicating His love and power in all circumstances.

16. Linked with other Christians involved in various areas of working for Christ.

17. Strongest when *weakest*. He or she has learned that strength comes from Christ and not found within oneself. He or she is able, willing, and ready to call upon Christ to fill one's life with His Spirit each day.

18. Filled with insight undetermined by man but given by the power of the Holy Spirit.

19. Willing to be prepared by God for a lifestyle discovered by a unique few. He or she has vowed to make Christ's way of life one's own, as Christ shows the way to travel the road of life.

20. Willing to admit mistakes and ready to ask forgiveness. *Will not* allow mistakes and errors to bring their faith to an end but will, instead, walk on with a renewed spirit.

21. Desires to please the living Lord.

22. Has a private time of devotion and prayer with Christ on a regular basis.

23. Carries a prayer in the heart and seeks to be in tune to Christ.

24. Inwardly *knows* that one must pursue the blueprint plan that Christ has set into place for him or her. Wants the challenges of the Christian life, not to please oneself, but to draw closer to our Lord, to know Him fully.

25. Has committed his or her life to Christ, and seeks to be holy, loving, caring, sharing, deeply committed to Christ—a person who reflects the qualities of life that Christ displayed while among us here on earth.

While you may not have all of these qualities, you may have a few or many of them. Let us use a scale to evaluate our present commitment to Christ such as the one below:

0–5   of the qualities—you have just begun.

6–9   a good beginning.

10–15   you're doing fine, press on and walk in faith.

16–20   Good for you! Press on faithful servant of Christ.

21–25   Be glad! You have discovered a quality of life that is worthy of sharing, a spirit-controlled life through the power of the living Christ.

All of us need to understand there is more to life after receiving the gift of salvation. There is *much* more to our Christian lives; Christ expects from us and commands us to reach out and be like Him. Conform to Christ's standards and be all you can be. Be someone who has found the glory of Christ in daily life and openly seeks to share the many joys of the abundant life with others.

QUALITIES TO ADMIRE IN THE LIFE OF PROMISE

When we consider qualities we admire in a person, what comes to mind first?

Loving.   Few of us function well without love in our lives. Love comes in many forms and is displayed in many ways. But what is the consistency of love offered through the Christ-led lifestyle? Surely Christ-like love should possess:

The Love of God.   Jesus said that through love all men would know that we are His disciples. (John 13:35) God's love is not selfish or self-seeking in thoughts or actions. It does not look out for its own interest first. God's love gives . . . it gives and gives and gives without ever expecting anything in return.

The love of God expects us to have and hold each other in special esteem. This love does not seek to edify itself but to uplift others through accepting others as they are today, tomorrow, and forever.

It is not easy for us to learn the deep truths of God concerning love. But as the Spirit directs us into new insights we quickly learn the value of life as God views it. Our investment of Christian love draws interest and reward which is deposited into our spiritual savings account. As we love others, as God loves us, "with no strings attached" then others may begin to alter their lifestyle and make steps to overcome feelings of being unacceptable or unworthy in the eyes of others. Learning to love as God loves comes under the direction of the Holy Spirit. We can learn it only through divine guidance and it is not developed within our own powers of reason. God's divine love is a mystery and is learned only as we gather opportunities presented by the Lord.

Love, God's way, takes time and willingness. It must be cultivated within our minds and our spirits. God's nature combined with our sense of reasoning often causes questions to arise. We find it difficult to love everyone and anyone. God's love, filtered through our spirit, brings lasting results which can bring another person into the reality that love is not selfish or self-seeking but is honest and open. 1 Corinthians 13, "The Love Chapter" of the New Testament tells us what love is and love is not. Reread it and discover some new insight which will show you the importance of loving in a Christ-like manner.

You know, love takes no account of the evil done it. It doesn't even keep score when someone abuses it or turns it away. Christ-like love ignores all the wrongs it has to suffer in the name of Jesus, as we share our faith, and forgive instantly. Love is more than a powerful tool in serving the Lord Jesus Christ, it is a way of life and we are commanded to walk in love through the power of the Holy Spirit in us.

Within the life of a truly committed Christian we see Christ's love reflected everywhere towards everyone. It is a love that is not hidden away but is displayed throughout the day. It does not grow stale or stagnant but grows more beautiful every day. Surely, this is the first quality we admire in those who serve Christ—love.

KNOWLEDGE AND WISDOM

Knowledge and wisdom are related and yet are not the same. You see, Christian friend, there are many who know the Word of God backward and forward. But they have never allowed it to melt the "icebergs of their cold and hardened hearts." Knowing something of the Scriptures does not necessarily mean that you have a complete understanding of God's message. Knowledge is good but wisdom is better.

- 1 Peter 2:2 has an important message for Christians, "Desire the sincere milk of the Word." The sincere milk of the Word gives understanding and meaning to Scriptures. While there are sincere people who never understand the Word of God, the person who vows to follow in the path of the Lord will learn, develop, and grow in their knowledge of the Scriptures.

Those who possess Godly knowledge know that it is presented to the sincere at heart. It is not given lightly but is given in various ways and associated with involvement and commitment. It comes not only to the pastor, teacher, or evangelist but also to those who desire enlightenment from God. The Holy Spirit is our teacher and our guide as we read, evaluate, and apply the Scriptures to our hearts. So it is with the wise Christian person, who knows the things that are of value and listens for the voice of God as they journey the pathway of life.

Wisdom is a gift from God. It is of great benefit to the believer in Christ. Throughout the Scriptures wisdom is spoken of frequently. Here are some verses which lend support to the value of wisdom:

- James 3:17 (NAS) "But the wisdom from above is first pure, then peaceable, gentle, reasonable, full of mercy, and good fruits, unwavering, without hypocrisy."

- Luke 21:15 (NAS) "I will give you utterance and wisdom which none of your opponents will be able to resist or refute."

- James 1:5 (NAS) "If any of you lacks wisdom, let him ask of God, who gives to all men generously and without reproach, and it will be given to him."

- Proverbs 2:6, 7 (NAS) "For the Lord gives wisdom; from His mouth comes knowledge and understanding. He stores up sound wisdom for the upright; He is a shield to those who walk in integrity."

Other verses concerning wisdom that you will find of interest are:

- Proverbs 16:16
- Proverbs 4:5–10
- Ecclesiastes 2:13; 7:12, 19; 9:18

The study of wisdom, as viewed in the Scriptures, is an exciting one. Consider wisdom from God's standards as a gift worth seeking. Do you see wisdom displayed in the life of the person you admire?

When we view the life of the dedicated but stumbling Christian let us not judge him or her harshly or unfairly. Let us view this person as God does, as someone who is building a stronger foundation for faith.

Life is not without problems and there may be no quick remedy when heartaches arise but despite it all, committed Christians have dedicated their lifestyle to development of a Christlike spirit. This investment is a worthy one, and one which will grow in value each day.

One of the chief obstacles which often arises, time and time again, is worldly opinions and striking remarks. Many people tend to shun or snub the person who seeks Christ's plan for life. They treat him or her differently, not understanding what motivates this person. And frequently the "neophyte" Christian is treated with indifference or ridiculed privately. It is not uncommon to be made fun of openly and privately. He or she is considered a "goody two shoes" or even worse "socially unacceptable" in the eyes of the world. I know this to be the truth for I have experienced it and know several other people who have been treated similarly. The world is blind to their goodness because they simply do not understand what makes faith function.

It isn't easy to overlook unkind remarks and eyes that glare at you from across the room but it can be done. Today's Christian has to take a stand not only for what is right but for your beliefs. There are even moments when you may be disliked and resented because of your commitment to Christ. The world would have us believe that promises and vows are unimportant and that Christ really doesn't expect us to live up to the standards set forth in the Scriptures. The Christian who seeks to please God will have to make some social sacrifices and turn away from things which might lead one into some of the marginal areas of life. The new Christian will have to make a decision concerning a worldly stand and whom to follow, the worldly system with its desires for things and position or Christ who will give us all we need both now and throughout eternity.

The Christian of today needs to decide where to stand. You will have to make important decisions and set your course. You can travel one of several roads:

COMMITMENTS OF FAITH IN THE FAMILY OF GOD

NOMINAL   LIMITED (Partial)   TOTAL

The nominal Christian lifestyle teaches: I am all important. I will fit Christ in when and wherever it is convenient. There are more important things in life than Christ, after all, I believe and that is what is important.

The limited Christian lifestyle teaches: some time for Christ, some for me, some for the family, and some for Christian involvement. While the partial commitment is stronger than the nominal Christian lifestyle, it has still not understood that Christ is to be number one in our lives. It still does pretty much as it pleases.

The total lifestyle teaches: Christ is number one in my life. It is Christ who helps me make the decisions, leads the way, and provides the blessings of life. It is a lifestyle that says, "yes" when Christ says, "I want you to be a part of my plan!"

The cost is high! The work of becoming a dedicated child of God is an ongoing experience but it is worth the investment. We must look at our lives and decide whom we live for and why. We can evaluate the life of the nominal Christian, the partial Christian, and the total Christian and consider the Godly person. How do we fit in? Are we involved in life as this person is involved? Have we seen the blessings and rewards as this person views them, or have we shunned Christ?

We often see so much in the Christ-like spirit of the dedicated Christian that we long for in our own lives. What it comes down to in making a commitment to life is this:

1. Do I want to develop the desirable qualities of the Christian life?

2. Am I willing to pay the price for the abundant life or will I hide away from Christ and ignore His call?

3. Have I considered the impact that Christ will allow my life to have on others when I pour my life into His?

4. Can Christ work through me and use me in a way that will bless my life and the life of others?

5. Do I radiate the love of Christ? Can others see the love I feel for Christ as I journey through life?

6. Am I willing to miss the rewards and blessings of my Christian life because I am too busy for Christ?

These questions can be answered as we evaluate our lives according to the qualities of the committed child of God. Go back a few pages and reread those twenty-five qualities of the Christian. Consider a Christ-led life as it stacks up against yours. Has God worked in your life to achieve His goals and purposes? Is He using you now as an instrument of love and service?

THE PERSON WHO WILL NOT MAKE PROMISES AND COMMITMENTS

We cannot close this chapter out without consideration of the nominal Christians who *will not* or *do not* make commitments to their faith. These people have no real commitment to faith or to Christ. They are unwilling to make promises for a variety of reasons and often make the excuse, "I'm just not ready to settle down yet."

They make no lasting impact on the Christian community and usually make excuses for not being involved in any Christian spiritual involvement. Such a person is a "Christian Dropout." You see, they dropped their commitment to trust and believe in the Lord with all of their heart, mind, and spirit. They are not investing time and efforts in eternal things, but look on the surface of life and live each day "to the fullest."

They are not obedient to God, but are flatly saying, "No, God, I do not want to have the qualities of a committed Christian person. No, God, I want to be what I want to be, not what you desire me to be." The fact is that they have spiritual *lethargy*. Pleasing their own desires and turning their backs on God, they lack a true inner spiritual strength.

God is not pleased when His children refuse Him. Time and time again He calls their names. He seeks to show them the error of their ways and yet many of them will never be more than nominal Christians. How sad it is to see wasted lives. And truly a life is wasted when it is lived outside Christ.

THINGS MISSED THROUGH A LACK OF COMMITMENT

What things are missed by the person who will not commit his or her ways to the Lord? I can only begin to relate them to you, but here are a few:

- No lasting contribution to furthering the faith and growing in the gift of grace God so richly gave through Christ.
- No worthy deeds or causes done that others might learn about Christ through your loving efforts.
- No deep fellowship with the Spirit.
- A lack of meaning and purpose to life.
- No understanding of God's gifts to those who believe.
- Rewards, blessings, gifts, and unspeakable joy which were held in reserve for you as a committed person of God.
- The loss of understanding Christ in a different light than you now see Him.

- Missing the power and the presence of the Spirit as He works in your life to help achieve God's plan for your life.

- Powerful influences given as a gift as you share your faith.

- The capacity to become more than you ever dreamed or thought you could be through the Spirit that lives within you.

- A feeling of achievement and self-worth as Christ allows you to serve in the spreading of the "good news."

- Total trust in Christ.

- Wisdom immeasurable by worldly standards.

There are thousands upon thousands of blessings missed due to the lack of keeping your vows or making important promises to the Lord. I can only tell you that if you refuse to commit your life to Christ you have missed a good portion of God's blessings for it is through sharing of our lives that life finds its greatest meaning.

Questions

1. What are three types of Christians as viewed in this chapter?
2. What is the purpose of commitment to Christ in our lives?
3. How does God view our vows of commitment to Him?
4. What are some of the differences we discover through commitment to Christ?
5. What is the challenge of commitment to today's Christian?
6. Name five blessings God has laid away for those who believe in Christ.
7. What is the most important truth, to you, concerning the Christ-centered person?
8. How does the world view Christ-centered people? Why?
9. What are some of the challenges of the Christ-centered person?
10. List eight ways we tend to view the Christ-led person.
11. What are some important facts concerning the life of a Christian?

12. What do those who refuse to make a commitment to Christ miss? Why?

13. Make a list of the people you most admire. What qualities in their lives make them a success? Why?

4
God's people of commitment

Don't allow the title of this chapter to scare you away. The message of this chapter is important to you and to me. You see, in learning to be God's people, we learn the value of life as it was intended to be, God's way. Understanding the privileges which accompany the responsibility of being truly "Godly" will allow us to determine the manner in which we should live.

It is not difficult for the Christian to become confused, as some available, admired leader describes how he or she thinks we *should* live and how we should respond to our Christian walk. Unfortunately, many of these misguided persons tend to lead you astray. Many of them set a standard which Christ has no desire for you to follow. They set out a structure which has worked for them, and their desire is for us to become carbon copies of them. You see, Christ never intended for us to become slaves to religious standards but to exercise our rights and freedom under His perfect direction. No wonder we tend to feel insecure and unwilling to become God's people. We have allowed someone else's standards to control our beliefs and determine our faith in Christ. Being godly is learned by becoming the person that God called you to be. Only our Lord has the plan-book which states the calling given you by Him. (Ephesians 2:10) NAS "For we are His worksmanship, created in Christ Jesus for good works, which God prepared beforehand, that we should walk in them." No human being has the right to make you conform to his or her rules or standards. We are to be as Christ wants us to be, nothing more—nothing less.

I hope this idea doesn't confuse you. I don't think it will. For you see it is by knowing who we are through the love of our Lord Jesus Christ that we become a usable vessel. No one should seek to mold us or bend us to their will for that is God's work. God is the potter, and we are lumps of clay. Sometimes within church circles, there are a few who seem to misdirect us, ever so slightly. By using selected biblical guidelines and then adding their own ideas and interpretations, they advise us that we should be this . . . we shouldn't be that. Actually they have become spiritual legalists seeking to limit us with rules, regulations, and standards set by their interpretation of "what they think." And yet there is little or no scriptural guidance from them to demonstrate how to live freely in Christ. This select group seems more determined to enslave our faith with legalism and less concerned about what course Christ has set for us. Each Christian life is molded differently, in order that we might use our spiritual gifts and talents to share our faith.

It seems that our efforts should concentrate on using the biblical guidelines and then applying those principles to our lives, not in scrambling around trying to conform to another human's standards. We serve Christ, not legalistic attitudes and patterns which seek to steal away our religious freedom. Recall, Christ came to free us from sin and the old way of life. His "Master Plan" is practical and sensible. So then, let us step out in the certain knowledge that the Christ-filled life allows us to gain the very essence of life through Him.

BELIEVE

For some of us, there was the opportunity to make a first-time commitment to believe that Christ is the Lord and Savior sent from God. For others there was a commitment to allow Christ to be the center of their lives. This commitment to Christ has lifted our spirits and allowed our hearts a reason to be joyous. Believing in Our Lord is the first step in becoming a person who will win victories in life through Jesus Christ. Here is a brief summary of our commitment to Christ as Lord of our lives.

To believe in Christ is to say

- I believe that the things Jesus taught are true. I know that when Jesus came to earth He dedicated His thoughts, teachings, actions, and ways to bring me into a full knowledge of God the Father.

- I believe that Jesus offered His life as a perfect sacrifice for me. Christ died so that my life need not be torn and shattered with sin. I believe that through Jesus Christ, life has meaning and purpose and without Him life is incomplete.

- I believe that my life can become complete through Christ. Christ as my Savior and Lord has shown concern, and the ultimate love for me, as an individual, through His dedication to God. I am worthy, through Christ, to be a child of God.

- I believe that Jesus Christ has shown me a better way to live. This "better way" is found by allowing myself to grow in knowledge and gain wisdom from drawing closer to Christ. Being one of God's people is what I desire to be for He teaches me to become a new person through a deeper understanding of Him. He will teach me, through the Holy Spirit, how to enjoy a life which has discovered the importance of following after Christ. I believe Christ has provided guidelines and established a plan for my life. This plan is available to me for the asking so that I might know how to be a Christ-led person.

- I believe that Christ can and will use me as a tool, a vessel, which will allow others to enter into a deeper relationship with Him. I believe that my life can be used to make a sizable impact on the life of another. I am assured that my life has purpose and meaning through Christ the Lord as I allow His spirit to move within me. I know the power and strength of Christ is my stronghold in life. When I am weak, Christ is strongest, for He is all powerful.

- I believe that I want to be godly because it is a gift which God has for me. I want to take this gift and use it, not to glorify myself or bring any attention to my life, but to gain the blessings of being an instrument of God. I want to be a person who knows, first hand, the truths of God as revealed to her by Him. I wish to know for myself the things which are of God and the things which are not. I believe that in learning them, for myself, that I can share them in a method which will bring glory to God and which will give my life a blessing through having been a person who knows and believes in Christ as Lord and Savior.

A PERSONAL CALL

Jesus Christ gives each of us an individual call to follow along with Him and to serve Him. He calls you by name. He tugs away at your heartstrings. You can almost hear His voice, "(your name), come along with Me. Allow me to show you a better way, a more inviting way to live each day of your life." When we understand this personal call from Christ, there must be a personal response on our part.

With the call of Christ you make a personal commitment to grow in faith, knowledge, understanding, and daily practice walking with Christ. There are certain questions which must be asked of one's self:

1. Do I want to be someone who seeks the Lord at all times?
2. Am I a willing follower or do I just follow halfway?

3. Am I willing to grow in the Word of God?

4. Am I willing to submit my old spirit for a renewed one?

5. Will I allow the Holy Spirit to teach my spirit?

6. Do I really want the satisfaction that comes from a closer relationship to Christ?

7. Am I ready to trust Christ to know what is best for me?

These are but a few of the questions you must ask yourself. Be honest with yourself! I believe you can say yes to each of these questions. For you see, I've been there and know the agony and the restlessness which fills your heart as you strive to answer all seven of these questions. I know what you feel in your heart. In fact, there were some of them I wasn't sure that I could say "yes, I will" to at all. But the Lord was kind and good to me and guided my heart to the understanding that I must at least try. You too can have that knowledge; give it a try. I know the fear of the unknown and perhaps the feeling that you could possibly fail which still lingers in your heart, but don't be discouraged. Jesus can and will make things right for you when you decide to follow Him all the days of your life.

I wasn't good enough. I wasn't capable of being God's Person or so I thought. I surely didn't know enough about the Bible or Christ and after all I really hadn't had the desire to learn. But now, things were different! I knew my time had come. I had to learn, for Christ was calling me. . . . "Come to Me." I could not imagine that Christ wanted me but I knew I needed Jesus, not just for today, but forever. I realized that my involvement with Christ would require a total commitment of my entire being. I understood that Christ desired the entire person not just the emotional part of me, but the thinking, working parts of me too.

I believed Christ had a better way. I heard His personal call to me. I trusted that, somehow, He would help me be the person He wanted me to be. I took the first step.

ALLOWING YOURSELF
FREEDOM THROUGH CHRIST

One of my major problems, as a growing Christian, seemed to be the existence of such a large variety of attitudes and beliefs. We are fed negative attitudes from our earliest childhood. You can't do that! You can't go there. You shouldn't be seen with so and so. You must not think certain thoughts, or talk a certain way. No wonder we shy away from making a total commitment to the Lord, we don't feel the committed Christian can do anything but sit around and frown. We don't know what we can and can't do because someone has spoken out giving us a slanted view of the Christian faith. What happens next is that we become confused and wander about spiritually seeking to know what is right.

What no one ever said is that we won't do many of those things we use to do anymore because we view life differently. Our focus shifts from worldly values to spiritual values. It isn't that we *can't* do these things, rather we *choose not* to do them! We are free, in Christ, to make our own choices and decisions. We begin to view life with new meaning. Something important has happened with our commitment to Christ—*old habits seem less important* than they were. Our grasp on wrong in our life begins to slip and fall away. The Holy Spirit helps us distinguish those things which are no longer important or good, and we begin to set them aside. We want a better way, and that way is found in Christ's examples of living. Instead of having to conform to the standards of the world, we make our own way through our new insight and understanding that we are adopted children of God.

Christ reveals things as they really are. Some are superficial and unreal. Some things are distorted and sinful, and yet a few things are very lovely. Some things even need to be changed.

They must be changed! You see much of what we have and do is for the approval of those around us. We want to be accepted by everyone. We want to be inside and a part of the good times, not on the outside seeking acceptance. Christ teaches us that He is what is important, not the desires of the world. He accepts us as we are and is pleased we are in the family of God. We no longer have to conform to someone else's standards or be a part of certain things to be accepted. Christ understands our needs and our hearts better than any one can and He accepts us in our torn-apart condition. He will guide us to other Christians who will respond to us as we are. You see, we Christians are not perfect, but Christ is! It is He who stands at the core of our lives, and it is He who gives us strength to overcome the adversaries of life. He knows what is an acceptable standard for each of us. In the companionship of other Christians we should discover our mutual love for Christ, our bond is Christ and not we ourselves. Within the Christian family we can know that Christ is among us. Christ lives in us and through us. We will sense a completeness by sharing our faith with one another and finding joy through Jesus. That is how Christ intended all things to be, united, complete, and whole.

In becoming committed to God you will want to use your gifts and talents in a useful manner. You need not hide yourself away but allow Christ to share His gifts through you. Let your life radiate the love of Christ. Your personality, your physical features, each mannerism you hold is a part of you. Have confidence and trust in the person you are. Use your spiritual gifts and talents wisely.

Accept yourself with the understanding that as your faith matures the unlovely things in your life will be altered. Put on a new attitude—I am a child of God, I am loved. Don't be afraid to be genuine. Be true to yourself knowing that He knows all about you and loves you. Love yourself as God has loved you.

You are the person God created to serve Him. He called you to become a "tool," a "vessel" which will bring honor to Him. Don't hide the real you, allow the light of Christ to shine within you. The light of Christ gives warmth and love as it spreads across the shadows of life.

I suppose that by now you have a slight hint that maturing in faith was a very real problem of mine in days gone by. Well, until I learned and accepted the fact that I needed to gain more knowledge of Christ's gift of salvation to me, I had little self-confidence. By allowing the light of Jesus to shine in the dark areas of my own life, I learned that He loved me no matter what my temperament, my personality, my troubles, or faults. Nothing could keep Christ from loving me. Furthermore, He showed me that He has a plan, an ongoing plan, for me to work in His fields to share the "good news" with others. Jesus wanted to use me! His call was to take the whole person, not just parts of me, and allow me to serve with Him. The call of Christ to serve Him is a life-changing experience.

Jesus Christ, my Lord, knew that when I accepted my personal call, the challenge to be one of God's people would show me how to overcome my personal handicaps through Him. Do you know what? He was right! Commit your problems to Christ for He cares for you. Allow Christ to guide you to a more complete life through a fuller understanding of Him. My weaknesses are His now. He has everything under control. "Or do you not know that your body is a temple of the Holy Spirit who is in you, whom you have from God, and that you are not your own? For you have been bought with a price: therefore glorify God in your body." 1 Corinthians 6:19, 20 (NAS)

To be committed to Christ, I must gain this attitude: "For not one of us lives for himself, and not one dies for himself; for if we live, we live for the Lord, or if we die, we die for the Lord; therefore whether we live or die, we are the Lord's." Romans 14:7, 8 (NAS) The key to life, Christian, is that we *are* the

Lord's. Accept this teaching from the Lord and allow it to strengthen your faith in Christ.

AFFIRM

Affirm that you are a follower of the Lord. Know that you are precious to Him. It is for our benefit that He came to earth and freed us from the grasp of sin and despair. Rejoice in knowing that He cares ever so much for you. Affirm your position in Christ, and allow yourself to be seen beside Christ on the cross. "I have been crucified with Christ; and it is no longer I who live, but Christ lives in me; and the life which I now live in the flesh I live by faith in the Son of God, who loved me, and delivered Himself up for me." Galatians 2:20 (NAS)

Affirm your trust. Do you trust Christ to know what is best for you? Do you block the efforts of the Holy Spirit to guide you each day? Do you quit trusting the Lord when the going gets tough? Do you really trust Christ with each area of your life knowing that He will see you through?

Trusting is learned by walking along the road of life with Christ. When you turn and run away from tests or trials then you are limiting the work of the Holy Spirit within you. To be a godly woman you must learn to stand firm and not run at the first sign of trouble. The Spirit will see you through good times and bad. The going might be tough but you can be assured that whatever happens is approved by God. The trials and sufferings may be painful and seemingly there is no escape, but Christ will not fail you. Whatever comes, no matter what, it is designed to bring you into a deeper relationship with the Lord. It is meant for you to understand and acknowledge your need for Christ to lead your life. It is only as you gain this trust and certainty that you will know the blessings of Christ.

KNOW

Christ has blessings and rewards for you. Not all blessings will be given here on earth but some await you in heaven. Although we may not know what they are—rest assured that they are known by the Creator and chosen just for you.

We do encounter earthly blessings from time to time. Have you experienced the joy of showing another the way to Christ? Did you see them become aware of their need for Christ as their Savior? Has a person who held an indifferent attitude toward you changed? Have you been a part of a group and shared something which helped another? Had the Lord given you a task to perform and the results were pleasing to you? Have you taken the opportunities which Christ has given you in your Christian walk?

We should know the blessings in this life are merely small rewards. It is in those moments when we think the Christian life is too difficult to live that we can begin to count our blessings. It isn't always easy to be a Christian, in fact there are moments when it is very difficult, but it is worth our effort. One moment of blessings outweighs months of struggles and conflict. The cost is high for commitment to Christ but the rewards are without measure. "Yes, indeed, I certainly do count everything as loss compared with the priceless privilege of everything, and value it all as mere refuse, in order to gain." (Williams) For it is through Christ that we have a life that is filled with purpose. Knowing that Christ's gift of salvation has come to you should surely be the greatest blessing of all.

BE TEACHABLE

My teacher friends tell me that it is often necessary to teach the same lesson several times before the student fully grasps the lesson. So it is with our Lord in His dealings with us! Sometimes, we are hard-headed people. We have to be taught the same lesson over and over. Time and time again, we stumble over the same problems. But a certainty is that we must be willing to be taught in order to be committed people. We must be receptive to change.

To overcome old habits and unusable characteristics in our lives, we must allow the Holy Spirit to instruct us. We must be willing to listen, and watch the Holy Spirit work in us as He strives to teach us how to overcome some of the wrong feelings and attitudes we have. Some of the areas in which the Holy Spirit will reveal the need for change in our lives are:

1. Lack of self control
2. Lying
3. Envy
4. Hate
5. Lust
6. Misguided desires
7. Fussing and fighting with others
8. Rebellion against authority
9. Rebellion that draws us away from Christ
10. Gossip
11. Cheating others
12. False pride
13. Enlarged egos
14. Fears
15. Uncontrolled anger
16. Resentments toward others
17. Lack of direction in our lives
18. Low self-esteem
19. Unflattering attitudes
20. Self-centeredness

Our list can grow quite lengthy. Looking at the list above will allow you to see that nothing that is really good for us will be given up when we make a full commitment to Christ. Christ takes the unattractive areas and changes them into something beautiful and good. After Christ alters the unlovely it is usable in our lives, for it has been altered and renewed by the power of Christ. Christ often allows His light to shine through us allowing us to display His love in our lives and be radiant persons of the living Lord.

GROW IN CHRISTIAN MATURITY

As we will learn in Chapter 6, there is a need for commitment to Christ. By combining our knowledge of Chapters 4 and 6 there should be no doubt as to our needs, desires, and goals in becoming one of God's people. Without a doubt, one of the least understood areas of the Christian life is the need to grow and mature in Christ. Most of us are not certain what steps need to be taken concerning our spiritual growth and progress.

For years, I had no idea that Christian maturity should be sought, let alone what it involved. I had never been taught this lesson or heard it discussed anywhere, but the fact was that I lived my life as a lazy Christian. I had expected to be fed the Word and yet never read it on my own. Sadly, I had depended entirely on someone else to feed me and give me spiritual nourishment as a Christian. I thought I had all that any other Christian had, and yet I still felt empty. What I was missing was the mark of maturity. I was a tiny baby in faith and surely very immature in action. I had not known that each Christian had the opportunity to grow in knowledge of Christ for I had not experienced it. I was spiritually limited by my lack of knowledge concerning spiritual things.

When I became aware of a need for Christian maturity, I wanted to learn more. My, what a surprise I had stored up for me! When I began to understand my need to grow and mature in my beliefs, then Christ began to teach me what was involved with commitment. I found I had a great deal to learn.

As a growing Christian, I became fully aware of my need to say no to some of my old habits. I had to give up some things which had not been good for me. I had to want a more mature relationship with the Lord before I could find it. With the maturing of my beliefs and the growing of my faith, the values of the Christian life were evident to me. Allow me to share with you some of my findings.

IMMATURE CHRISTIANS

I was an immature Christian. I didn't know that I was but I was, and when I learned this truth there were decisions I had to make:

1. Continue on my present course.
2. Seek changes in my life.
3. Commit myself to a fuller understanding of my faith.
4. Turn away and fall away from the faith I had in Christ.

Since I was unwilling to turn completely away from my faith and trust in Christ, the field of choices was narrowed. I could not, now that I understood the need for change, continue on my present course. I had to make changes. I wanted to make changes, but commitment would be necessary to understand the Scriptures and my beliefs in Christ as Lord and Savior. My awakening caused me to make responsible decisions. It was necessary to create a new environment in which to develop my understanding of the Christian's commitment to life.

SPIRITUAL IMMATURITY

Spiritual immaturity is a result of the lack of not knowing the Word of God for one's self. It is only as we make a concentrated effort to read and study the Bible that we can grow in understanding. Effort is the key to progress, linked with a sincere heart's desire to know and experience God in your life. Actually it is fun and exciting to read the Bible.

It is my hope that we can rid our lives of inaccurate thinking and responses as we mature in faith. Look at the words of the Apostle Paul concerning spiritual immaturity within the church at Corinth. "So I myself, brothers, could not deal with you as spiritual persons, but as creatures of human clay, as merely baby Christians. I fed you with milk not solid food, for you could not take it. Why you cannot take it even now, for you are still unspiritual. For when there are still jealousy and wrangling among you, are you not still unspiritual and living by human standard?" 1 Corinthians 3:1–4 (Williams)

We must desire to grow from spiritual babies to mature adults. To achieve maturity we will grow through various stages of development. First, as babies, we will be the milk of the word, spiritual understanding. Yet we will be growing through the understanding that we already have while we seek more.

Second, we become young children in our maturity. We are beginning to age a bit. We have begun to see that a personal relationship with Christ is most important in our lives. We still have a tendency to behave like children in our actions, acting childish in some areas of our lives. We grow a little each day but we are making continual progress. Some of the actions and mannerisms we have which may still be childish are:

1. Pouting when we don't have our way.
2. Fits of anger.
3. Fighting (physical).

70

4. Arguing with others that we might have our way.

5. Anxiousness to point out someone else's faults.

6. Speech patterns—hurting others with words that lash out in anger.

We might want to pause for a moment and remember the words of Paul. 1 Corinthians 13:11 (Williams) "When I was a child, I talked like a child, I thought like a child, I reasoned like a child. When I became a man, I laid aside my childish ways." Just to be truthful about the entire matter—many Christians have yet to lay aside their childish ways. You see them all about you and especially in the fellowship of churches. They have to be the center of attention and they often make a lot of noise to gain that attention. They want their way and are very vocal about it when they don't have it. They behave like little children, and Paul clearly teaches us that when we grow up—mature—we are to lay aside those old habits and attitudes which are childish. You see, we are new persons in Christ. We aren't to behave like children and that is clearly stated. He expects us to change our old ways, the unlovely ways, and seek the attitudes which reflect Christ in our lives. The results are pleasing not only to us but to those who know us.

The sad fact is that you and I can never become God's persons of commitment until we pack away our old attitudes. We must grow in faith and mature in wisdom. The only way to do that is to rid your life of old, unlovely attitudes.

The next stage of spiritual growth is the young adult stage. We begin to gain new knowledge of God through our studying and feasting on the "meat" of the Word. The meat is found in understanding the Scriptures which lead us to deal with the truths of God. It is taking the Word of God, reading it, studying it, and learning what God has for you to learn.

The adult stage of Christian growth is our goal. We must grow and become strong in the Word of God. It is necessary for us to pray, read, study, listen, and allow the Holy Spirit to work through us. As maturing Christians we will want to have the "meat" of the Word as a continual part of our growth process. A steady diet of spiritual meat is necessary to cause proper growth and to make us strong in the Word of God. We find we are no longer satisfied with milk, we need something which will fill our spirits and satisfy our souls. The pure meat of the Word is intended to bring this satisfaction. Being God's person of commitment will bring us into the understanding that we need this solid food, each day, and we will seek it to nourish our hearts and satisfy our souls.

Let's set aside spiritual immaturity and set out to reach the goal of the maturing of our faith. Let's learn to exercise our spiritual insight and share what we have with others.

SPIRITUAL MATURITY

As we have mentioned the goal of the spiritual adult is the gaining of wisdom and maturity through further knowledge of Jesus Christ. As we mature we have certain responsibilities. Let's look for instruction on this matter from the Scriptures.

- Hebrews 5:11b–14 (Williams) "Since you have become so dull in your spiritual senses. For although you ought to be teachers of others because you have been Christians so long, you actually need someone to teach you over and over again the very elements of the truths that God has given us, and you have gotten into such a state that you are in constant need of milk instead of solid food. For everyone who uses milk alone is inexperienced in the message of right-doing; he is only an infant. But solid food belongs to full-grown men who on account of constant use have their faculties trained to distinguish good and evil." We can almost say, "Ouch!" to this series of passages. For some of us it is as though the writer of Hebrews was peering over our shoulder and probing our consciences. He clearly shows us as we are and as we should be. He wants us to know the truth of God. He desires that we know how to distinguish good and evil in our Christian adventure. It is through maturity!

- Ephesians 4:13–15 (NIV) "Until we all reach unity in the faith and in the knowledge of the Son of God and become mature, attaining to the whole measure of the fullness of Christ. Then we will no longer be infants, tossed back and forth by the waves, and blown here and there by every wind of teaching and by the cunning and craftiness of men in their deceitful scheming. Instead, speaking the truth in love, we will in all things grow up into him who is the Head, that is, Christ." Becoming mature people of God will give our lives stability. We will no longer be tossed to and fro by all manner of doctrines and schemes to sidetrack us from discovering the radiance of the Lord at its fullest. We will grow up and bear the certain knowledge that being Christ's committed people is the greatest reward of all. To be used of the Lord and to serve Him in a fullness of spirit will allow us to experience the greatest joy of all—being secure in Christ.

- 2 Corinthians 9:6–11 (Williams) "Now this is the way it is: Whoever sows sparingly will reap sparingly too, but whoever sows bountifully will reap bountifully too. Each must give what he has purposed in his heart to give, not sorrowfully or under compulsion, for it is the happy giver that God loves. And God is able to make your every spiritual blessing overflow for you, so that you will always have in every situation an entire sufficiency and so overflow for every good cause; as the Scriptures say: 'He has generously given to the poor, His deeds of charity go on forever.' He who always supplies the sower with seed and the eater with bread will supply you with seed and multiply it and enlarge the harvest which your deeds of charity yield. In every way you will grow richer and richer so as to give with perfect liberality, which will through me result in thanksgiving to God for it."

There, Christian friend, is the very essence of life—give what you have, generously, with a glad heart. Giving includes not only your money but your time, talents, gifts, abilities, your *Christian love*, your faith, and your all for the work of the Lord. He will give you the seeds to sow where they need to be sown. He will give you spiritual blessings for your efforts. He will supply all you need to carry through each task and even more than all these; He is a part of your life.

The guidelines for being God's committed people are simple, and yet very few of us have the courage to accept the challenge. Being God's person of commitment will bring our lives into a deeper faith, a growing maturity, and a life filled with blessings. The decision is before you:

1. Accept the challenge and adventure of being God's total person, or

2. Reject the plan that God has for you to be a usable vessel of His.

It is my prayer that you will pray over this matter. Reread this chapter and decide for yourself what you really desire from life. The guidelines are here but they will be useless unless you apply them to your life. It takes courage to become and be all that Christ wants you to be, but as the Scriptures teach us, "God is able to make your every spiritual blessing overflow. . ." Allow that idea to become a reality in your life. Step forward and accept the challenge of God's personal call for you. "Come, follow Me!"

Questions

1. What are the various stages of spiritual growth?

2. How do we gain additional insight concerning spiritual growth?

3. What questions must we ask ourselves concerning commitment to Christ?

4. How do old habits change through our commitment to Christ?

5. Why is this necessary?

6. How should we consider our blessings from God and why should we consider them in this manner?

7. What are six areas of your life where changes are needed to further your spiritual growth?

8. What are some of the characteristics of the immature Christian?

9. What are some of the characteristics of the mature Christian?

10. Once you see the need for change, what steps should you take?

11. What is the most important truth you have learned in this chapter?

5

Fears, doubts, and trusting

Negative feelings and attitudes limit our potential and imprison our abilities to experience a successful personal relationship with Christ. We must be careful not to allow the negative to drive a wedge of doubt and fear in our way of life.

Some of our old habits are hard to break. Because this is true, we encounter "spiritual setbacks" as we journey the road of life. Some of our old habits will need to be set aside as we vow to be a Christ-led person. Afflictions caused by doubts and fears might render us inoperable and that is the last thing any committed Christian wants to happen to their life.

PATTERNS OF DOUBT

"I doubt if God can use me because . . .," "If only I hadn't . . .," "If only I had . . .," "But you don't know me, the kind of person I really am . . .," "I'm not worthy of . . . and besides God wouldn't want to use somebody like me; I just can't do anything spiritual, it's just not in me." There are a variety of excuses we form as we consider ourselves unworthy to work for the Lord. For the most part, our doubts and fears are caused by a lack of self-confidence and security. Perhaps we don't see our positive side because we have failed somewhere in our past.

The truth is we are involved in spiritual conflict as we strive to serve Christ. Perhaps now, with the Holy Spirit in control of the situation, we will find victory. We apply His strength to our situation and He will see us through difficult times and will deliver us from our encounter with doubt. He will allow us to view our weaknesses as they are, momentary spiritual setbacks designed to draw our interests elsewhere. The Holy Spirit will direct us into knowledge that Christ desires us to turn aside the negative and immerse our lives in His plan for our lives.

When doubts arise and we find ourselves wading ankle deep in despair and fear, it is time to abandon ship. We need a more seaworthy vessel which will keep us safe throughout the storms of life. Christ allows the total person with his ambitions, dreams, doubts, heartaches, unbelief, desires, strengths, and weaknesses to find a secure life through an indepth knowledge of Him in His ship of life.

I SHALL NOT DOUBT

That's easier said than done, isn't it? I shall not doubt myself as a usable vessel in the family of God. I shall accept myself, as I am, knowing the Spirit will change those things which are weaknesses and give me strength through His Spirit. I must learn that Christ will bear positive results in my life as I witness to other people. The negative feelings shall no longer cause spiritual stagnation for I know in whom I believe, and I belong to Him.

When I discover the feelings of doubt, my most effective weaponry is the Word of God implanted in my life by the Holy Spirit. "Finally, my brethren, be strong in the Lord and in the power of His might. Put on the whole armor of God, that you may be able to stand against the wiles of the devil. For we do not wrestle against flesh and blood, but against principalities, against powers, against the rulers of the darkness of this age, against spiritual wickedness in the heavenly places. Therefore take up the whole armor of God, that you may be able to withstand in the evil day, and having done all, to stand." Ephesians 6:10–13 (NKJV)

As we consider the ineffectiveness that doubts cast in our lives we realize who the authors of many of our doubts are:

- the wiles of the devil
- principalities
- powers
- rulers of the darkness
- spiritual wickedness in the heavenly places

No wonder we have our hands full handling our doubts and fears. Our lives are involved in a tremendous struggle not only with our own spirit, but with the spirit of outside forces. Here are some new ideas I formed as I understand doubt in my life.

1. I cannot overcome doubt and spiritual forces without Christ.
2. The Holy Spirit can show me how to walk by the Spirit. (Galatians 5:16–26)
3. I must be led by the Holy Spirit in all areas of my life, especially in those areas where I am weakest. (Romans 8:14)
4. Doubts steal away peace, joy, happiness, the very fruit of the Spirit which I seek to have for my own.
5. In doubtfulness it is difficult to please God.
6. I must learn to live by faith. (1 John 5:4; Romans 5:1; Galatians 2:20)

7. Doubt drives a wedge between my confidence and my trust in Jesus when it is allowed to wander on its own.

DOUBTS BREED FEAR

Doubts and fear lead to failure unless given to the Lord. Fear need not drag us downward to the level of lack of accomplishment or low achievement in our lives. The only way to overcome our fear is through Christ. We have to reach out for His outstretched hand and make contact with Jesus by faith, and believe that He will overcome our doubts and fear.

Allow me to share an example of real fear and fright from the life of our son, Ray, who went to camp with his fifth grade class. Because of a past experience with storms and a fear of tornadoes Ray's fear grew stronger as storms rolled through the area. The springtime thunderstorm rumbled through the area shaking the windows of Ray's cabin. Ray's thoughts were, "I was so scared I didn't know what to do! My counselor finally took me to the teacher's cabin. I stayed there a while and talked to them. I was a little scared because you weren't here to take care of me, Mom."

When I asked Ray what happened in the teacher's cabin he smiled and replied, "Well, we just sat around and talked a while. Mrs. Dane (one of the fifth grade teachers and a fine Christian woman) talked to me about faith and trusting in Jesus. Since she knew I was a Christian we talked a little about faith and that kind of thing. As she talked to me, I remembered the Bible in my pack and I went back to my cabin and took it out and read it. All those things you had underlined really stood out and caught my eye. I wasn't as afraid as I had been, and I knew Jesus was with me. And," he said with a big grin, "I slept with my Bible under my pillow. It made me feel better and I wasn't as afraid as I was."

Ray's fear had almost overcome him when the storms came through the area, but he was able to overcome his fear through Christian schoolteachers who cared for him and loved him with the love of Christ. Brenda (Mrs. Dane) told me about Ray's fear: She said, "He really was scared! I did everything I could to comfort him and help him and since I knew Ray was a Christian it was pretty easy to calm his fears."

"You know, Brenda," I replied, "I told Ray that when he went to camp a legion of angels was going with him. I figured he needed more than one, so I asked the Lord to send a legion along for the ride and I'm sure He kept them all busy."

Brenda's reply was almost comical: "I believe they put in some overtime and I'm sure they got a good workout." Ray's fear of storms almost overwhelmed him, but the Spirit supplied Ray's needs through a Christian friend.

While Ray's fear of storms is not entirely gone, it is being overcome through understanding that we all have fears and the Spirit is teaching all of us how to deal with the weak areas in our lives. It is my prayer that someday soon Ray's fear of storms will diminish. I know that his faith is growing as each day passes and his concept of the Holy Spirit as His protector grows.

FEARS

Each life has a specific purpose and it takes time to learn God's will and to apply it to our daily living situations. An honest examination of fear will reveal some important facts concerning our faith or lack of faith. It's time to face up to the facts concerning our fears and eliminate many of them through this process. It's time to grow up in Christ and mature in faith.

Some of the things which cause fears are:

- Indecision in our lives
- Burdens which seem overwhelming
- Low self-esteem
- Worry
- Superstitions
- Trauma in our lives
- Pain
- Stress
- Shyness
- Loneliness
- Bitterness
- Confusion
- Emotional disturbances
- Lack of security
- Unpleasant experiences from the past
- Unbelief
- Lack of faith and trust

Various stages of fear can cause us to make some strange choices in our lives. Will we allow the fear to overtake our spirit, or will we allow Jesus an opportunity to overcome our weaknesses in His power? The choice is ours. God is eternally interested in our problems and needs. Giving them to Him is our personal vote of confidence. Will He see us through? Of course He will! After all is said and done, there is no one person who can make any of us any stronger in our faith except our Lord. The Lord waits, patiently, to direct us into deeper understanding concerning our walk of faith. By trusting Him in times of stress we gain a lasting calmness and a peace that is unshakable. Ours is to trust Christ in *all* things, each moment we live. He has promised to supply our needs according to His abundant grace, and He keeps His promises.

PLEASING GOD

We cannot please God through fearful attitudes and reactions. Because we have quenched the free flow of the Holy Spirit in us, He restrains Himself and lets us try to work at solving our own problems. Our secret (and not so secret) fears cause negativeness. Negativeness if not dealt with can become a way of life that will keep us from experiencing the complete peace of the Christian life. We have to surrender our negative way of life and let God show us how to be happy by thinking positively.

Please God by trusting in Christ. Don't bind yourself to doubts, frustration, fear, and an over-demanding spirit. Don't be a "spiritual turtle" afraid to stick your head out of your shell. Allow Christ to teach you what trusting means. Here are some of the points I have discovered in trusting Christ and setting wrong attitudes aside:

1. Pretending doesn't work. I had to learn to be honest about my life, myself, and my needs. Be real, be honest, be the person you were created to be. And I learned that the person I really was really wasn't such an awful person at all. That gave my life a renewed spirit of hope and promise.

2. Trust Christ. Allow His Spirit to flow through you. When we fully trust Jesus, Lord of all things, then we ease the stress and burden of unnecessary worry. Christ takes away those things which hinder us from having a productive life. He replaces them with a more secure feeling. An attitude of peace and calmness throughout the day is ours because we have the unspeakable calmness of the Holy Spirit continually working in our lives.

3. We please God by gaining a boldness of spirit. We are no longer

"spiritual turtles" sneaking a peek at the world. Become aware of God's promises and begin to apply them to each situation which causes you problems. You will quickly learn to gain confidence in Christ and allow Him the honor of showing you how to overcome the most adverse of circumstances.

4. We please God by making a personal commitment to Him and sticking with it. We do not make a promise today and deny it tomorrow. We learn to stand firm saying, "I can do all things through Christ who strengthens me."

There are many Scriptures which can build our confidence, give us encouragement, and enlighten our spirit. Let's look at a few of them and consider the Word of God as it speaks to our hearts.

- Psalms 84:11 (NAS) "For the Lord God is a sun and a shield; the Lord gives grace and glory; no good thing does He withhold from those who walk uprightly."

In this Scripture we gain some valuable insight into God's character and our relationship to Him as His children. He is our sun and our shield. Consider how important the sun is to our daily existence; without it we would quickly perish. He is our warmth and the giver of life. He is our provider and our shield of blessings throughout each day. What words of encouragement and delight. Our spirits should be lifted as we gain knowledge of God through this Bible verse.

When we allow doubt and fear to have their way we can miss many of the blessings of God. Because we have allowed the negative to rule our lives we do not walk uprightly in a godly manner. The negative factors take us along a crooked path and lead us away from the good things of God.

As we become aware of the facts concerning negativeness we have taken the first steps to overcome it. Surely we want to walk uprightly so that we might experience the fullness of His loving Spirit, and we can change our ways. The roads we travel with Him are straight and sure. There are no crooked paths to lead us astray.

- Psalms 118:5–8 (NAS), "From my distress I called upon the Lord; the Lord answered me and set me in a large place. The Lord is for me; I will not fear; What can man do to me? The Lord is for me among those who help me; Therefore I shall look with satisfaction on those who hate me. It is better to take refuge in the Lord than to trust in man."

I Will Fear Not. Why? Because the Lord is for me! Well, nothing is too powerful for the Lord Jesus Christ to overcome because He is the Almighty God. *Always remember that!*

The almighty Lord is for me. He stands firm and does not waver or run away when trouble comes to us. He does not fear anything or anybody. In moments of stress He answers our call for help. He is our perfect refuge and protection from the storms of life. Since we, as believers, are a part of the family of God then He strengthens our hearts. He lifts our spirits. He gives us hope in those moments when we feel we cannot go on.

Surely the negative forces in life have no hold on us as we apply these Scriptures with complete understanding to our situations. His vows are firm. He stands as true and as strong today as He did in the time of Moses, Abraham, Noah, Paul, and so many more. He shows us how not to fear when the storms come; as he did with the saints of old, He will see us through.

- 1 Peter 5:6, 7 (Williams) "Therefore humbly submit to God's strong hand, so that at the proper time He may exalt you. Cast every worry you have upon Him, because He cares for you."

As Christians, we have so many blessings through Christ and for the most part many of us tend to neglect them. When we submit our minds, our hearts, and our spirits to His perfect guidance our lives are renewed and refreshed. He has promised to care for us, to take our worries, to provide for our real needs, and to keep us as His own. So why not let Him? We should not neglect to apply God's promises and erase many years of doubt due to our wavering faithfulness. Look at what this Scripture teaches us.

When we submit to God's guidance, He will exalt us. Consider the depth of that statement for just a minute or two. He has promised to lift us up, glorify us. And what have we done to deserve such an honor from God? Merely believe and trust in Christ. Much like a gift, given us freely and unrestricted, we receive honor because we allow Christ to work in our lives. Our promise to follow Him, to be His, to commit our lives to Him, has not gone without notice.

He wants to show us how deeply He cares for us and most of us are too busy doing something else to listen to the voice of the Lord as it speaks to our hearts. No wonder we feel something is missing in our lives, we have not applied the promises of God in a realistic fashion in our lives. We cast our cares on Him and what does He do? He lifts us up! He gives us an unshakable security and a life that is filled with His loving concern.

What more could we need or want in our lives than to know the fullness of the Lord? As we experience His complete love and the fullness of the abiding life, our fears are driven away. We become devoted to Christ not because we have to, but because we want to. We should realize that His commitment to us, as believers, is the highest honor given to mankind. His commitment began long ago and will stand until the end of time. What a blessed people we are! Our blessings multiply and expand as we believe, trust, and apply Christ's promises each day we live.

Questions

1. What do fears and doubts do to our Christian walk of faith?
2. How important is it to set aside the negative forces in life and look to the positive nature of Christ?
3. What are your deepest doubts concerning your life?

4. What fears maintain some control in a part of your life today?

5. How can you set aside fears and doubts when they arise?

6. As a Christian why is it important for you to place total trust in Jesus Christ?

7. Why do the promises of Christ stand strong and firm?

8. What do the words, "Be strong in the Lord and in the power of His might," mean to you?

9. Whose strength do you rely on most, your own or Christ's? Why?

10. How is Christ able to overcome our weaknesses?

11. Can fear render you useless as a usable vessel of God?

12. How does worry contribute to a lack of complete faith and trust in the Lord?

13. What can be done to overcome these attitudes?

14. Locate five Scripture promises which encourage you to draw on the strength of Christ for your daily needs. Write them in your notebook.

15. How can you please God? Do you want to please Him?

6

A commitment to grow in faith

As we have seen throughout our study, commitment takes effort. This chapter concentrates on our commitment to grow in faith. Growing in faith comes not only by allowing our faith to grow but also by being actively involved in the development of our faith.

Our faith was designed to be an active involvement in the sharing of our beliefs in Christ as our Lord and Savior. For many of us, faith seems to stand still, while others experience a deep seated faith which grows strong and sturdy. What happens when we encourage our faith to reach for new heights? It grows stronger and better. Why is commitment to our faith important? Why is it necessary to expand our faith?

The questions above are not easily answered. They can, in fact, cause us to make decisions and commitments which have previously been ignored by many of us.

WHY IS COMMITMENT
TO OUR FAITH IMPORTANT?

Without a commitment to trust and believe in Jesus Christ, our faith will fall short. We seek to compromise Christ's standards to suit our needs while we ignore His will for our lives. We will learn very quickly that this won't work and it is wrong thinking.

Without commitment to a personal faith there is only a passing dedication to Christ. We may find ourselves trying to live outside of our Christian standards and faith to please ourselves, and that just isn't practical Christianity. If we have no personal commitment to Christ there is no discipline or desire to read our Bible and apply the teaching to our lives. Our beliefs are not consistent, and we may even neglect the opportunity to listen for instruction and leadership from the Holy Spirit. Without a full commitment to our faith we will not:

- Read the Bible.
- Study the Scriptures.
- Pray.
- Meditate on God's value system.
- Or seek to gain guidelines on how to walk with Him.

These ideas should be a part of our Christian adventure. But for many of us they are not worthy of our consideration, for we live a carnal Christian life and do not seek after the spiritual aspects of our faith. When we view our lives as they are, we quickly find that each individual Christian is responsible for his own decisions. We decide the course we will take and whom we will follow. We decide how important our faith and trust in Christ really are, and we live by our decisions. A successful Christian life depends on the choices we make today, and the time is at hand for us to choose our course. It is my hope that we will make our decisions of commitment wisely and not turn away from the Lord.

90

TURNING AWAY

Through our personal commitment to Christ we will seek to turn away from the unpleasing areas of life. We will strive to seek a new nature, one pleasing to the Lord and to ourselves. We will want to rid our lives of the spiritual garbage which has gathered in our old carnal nature and live a more beautiful lifestyle. We will *want* Christ in the center of our lives because we know His ways *are* better than ours.

We must have a willingness to move away from old habits and ungodly desires of the sinful nature. Some of the areas we must be willing to surrender are:

1. Lower, earthly nature
2. Sexual immorality
3. Immorality
4. Impurity
5. Passion
6. Evil desire
7. Greed
8. Anger
9. Rage
10. Malice
11. Abusive, filthy talk
12. Lying

The above list is found in Colossians 3:5–9 (Williams). The Bible also tells us to "practice occupying our minds with the things above, not with the things on earth." Colossians 3:2 (Williams) It does take a form of dedication to rid ourselves of all the unpleasant attitudes and thoughts that dominate our lives. This attitude should lead us to deeper Christian principles bearing in mind,

"For He delivered us from the domain of darkness, and transferred us to the kingdom of His beloved Son, in whom we have redemption, the forgiveness of sins." Colossians 1:13, 14 (NAS) Our reasons for a full commitment of our faith all rest in the Lord Jesus Christ and our relationship to Him. We are partakers of His grace. We should live our lives with the understanding that He has only the greatest concern for us. We are important to Him and in time we gain a certain knowledge that faith in Christ is limitless.

WHY IS IT NECESSARY TO EXPAND IN FAITH?

We expand our beliefs so we may grow and mature in faith. Persons who do not progress in the Christian adventure simply goes nowhere. Their faith is limited in scope and perspective. They will not find the security of faith that is gained through experiencing faith at work each day. By expanding our faith, our understanding of commitment grows.

Think with me, for a moment, of the words of the Apostle Paul, "For I am convinced that neither death, nor life, nor angels, nor principalities, nor things present, nor things to come, nor powers, nor height, nor depth, nor any other created thing, shall be able to separate us from the love of God, which is in Christ Jesus our Lord." Romans 8:38, 39 (NAS) This is the kind of security you and I want and need. It allows our faith to become certain and we will, without hesitation, understand the things which are ours because Christ lives in our hearts. We must not allow our faith to be quenched. We have to learn to overwhelmingly conquer through Him who loved us, so that we might experience the abundant life. We must expand our faith so we will truly understand our Lord's love for us.

If we don't begin to expand our faith in Christ, we might

simply miss the very essence of life. Christ gives life, "new life." "Do not conform to this world, but be transformed by the renewing of your mind, that you may prove what the will of God is, that which is good and acceptable and perfect." Romans 12:2 (NAS)

I am fearful that many of us have already lost heart and courage. We have become discouraged and turned away from our pursuit of the glory of God as revealed in Christ Jesus. Our faith is to progress, not to stand still; we should be ever changing by growing deeper and stronger each day. Our faith must direct us toward a closer relationship with Christ. Each day's progress should be made bringing us to the reality that we are to "walk in a manner worthy of the calling with which we have been called, with all humility and gentleness, with patience, showing forbearance to one another in love." Ephesians 4:1b, 2 (NAS)

Why expand our faith? So we might guide others along the rough spots they encounter through our efforts to share a part of their burdens. By sharing our experiences we help others who struggle in desperate situations, find answers to problems, and develop lasting friendships. As we exercise our faith it enlarges and we receive an abundance of blessings from God. And most important of all, the sharing of our faith encourages others to make a deeper commitment of faith to Christ.

WHAT HAPPENS AS FAITH GROWS?

What won't happen would be a better question! Everything changes. Not only does my self-confidence grow but my entire outlook on life begins to change. The more I allow my faith to develop and work, the more I see Christ in my life.

Listen, Christian friend, when I begin to give up:

- self-centeredness

- selfish desires
- wrong motives and attitudes
- wrong relationships
- bad habits
- unspiritual thoughts

I begin to seek the righteousness of the Lord. Then things change for the better. I begin to see how the attitudes of a lifetime need to be altered, and become aware that my relationship with Christ has not been honest.

As I awaken my desire to become a *true* believer and complete follower of Christ, I must ask myself:

1. Am I willing to commit to Christ my entire day?
2. What does my heart really feel about Christ?
3. Does my life reflect the love of Christ?
4. Am I concerned enough for others to help them?
5. Do I really believe the teachings of Christ?
6. Do I take more from life than I give to it?
7. Am I willing to change wrong attitudes?
8. Do I want my faith to grow?

I must take an honest look at my life and answer the questions listed above. Some of my answers may reveal a few startling facts concerning my Christian life. I have not committed my life fully to Christ and have been living very selfishly. I am a taker of blessings and seldom a giver of anything in return.

Honest answers reveal our need to grow in our understanding of Jesus Christ as Lord of our lives. When we adjust our attitudes and spread our faith around, we will become aware of the hidden blessings of the Christian life.

How, you ask, could there be a blessing in placing others first? Well, I used to ask the same thing. But you see we are instructed to consider others as more important than ourselves. "If you have any encouragement from being united with Christ, if any comfort from his love, if any fellowship with the Spirit, if any tenderness and compassion, then make my joy complete by being like-minded, having the same love, being one in spirit, and purpose. Do nothing out of selfish ambition, or vain conceit, but in humility, consider others before yourselves. Each of you should look not only to your own interests, but also to the interest of others. Your attitude should be the same as that of Christ Jesus." Philippians 2:1–5 (NIV)

You see, it is in being properly concerned for others that we find fulfillment in our lives. The more we focus our attention on the needs of others, the more we will find our happiness and joy in Christ. Being concerned and truly caring for someone else is a true exercise of our Christian love and faith. Because of a genuine expression of love and an unselfish desire to help others, we learn the true meaning of Christian love—others first, self last.

- Romans 12:9–16 (NIV) gives further information on the sharing of our love through our expression of faith, "Love must be sincere. Hate what is evil; cling to what is good. Be devoted to one another in brotherly love. Honor one another above yourselves. Never be lacking in zeal, but keep your spiritual fervor, serving the Lord. Be joyful in hope, patient in affliction, faithful in prayer. Share with God's people who are in need. Practice hospitality. Bless those who persecute you; bless and do not curse. Rejoice with those who rejoice; mourn with those who mourn. Live in harmony with one another. Do not be proud, but be willing to associate with people of low position. Do not be conceited." There are few verses that share the essence of our expression of faith like this passage. And through our understanding we have tremendous opportunity to serve the Lord by sharing our faith with others.

SELF

"Do not think of yourself more highly than you ought, but rather think of yourself with sober judgment, in accordance with the measure of faith God has given you." Romans 12:3b. What measure of faith has God given you? How deep does your faith go? How limited is your faithfulness to Christ in an uncomfortable situation?

I believe these are questions that must be dealt with as individuals are called by Christ. Your answer won't be the same as mine, for the measure of our faith is known only to God. Christ has given each of us the proper measure needed to carry us through our Christian life. It's ours for the asking and is always functioning in an effort to help us overcome evil with goodness— if only we will accept it.

You see, our faith is only limited by our own worst enemy— self. My self can be my best friend or my strongest enemy. How I am willing to respond to God's call depends on nothing more than self. What is self willing to do? What does self run from? What is more important, self or my Lord? Does my self live as Paul . . . "I have been crucified with Christ and I no longer live, but Christ lives in me. The life I live in the body, I live by faith in the Son of God, who loved me and gave himself for me." Galatians 2:20, 21a. Self must learn that it is Christ who leads the way in my life.

Life has its greatest value when we learn that through keeping our promises to Him we gain and function without hindrances. It is through Christ that we gain confidence and trust for living each day. By experiencing Christ's full love we have a confidence that we shall abound and prosper even more. We are His followers, His servants to further His work as He opens the doors of life. We find the full assurance of life in Christ as we strive to serve Christ, the author of our salvation.

Christ gives life. He gives it to those who will accept the call. With your commitment to lead a Christ-filled life, there are unspeakable treasures awaiting you. They cannot be bought with silver or gold, but have been paid for by Him at the cross. Even though the road may be a bit rough and we grow weary, there is something special about having full confidence in Christ.

- "I can do all things through Him who strengthens me." Philippians 4:13 (NAS)
- "Finally, brethren, whatever is true, whatever is honorable, whatever is right, whatever is pure, whatever is lovely, whatever is of good repute, if there is any excellence and if anything worthy of praise, let your mind dwell on these things. The things you have learned and received and heard and seen in me, practice these things; and the God of peace shall be with you." Philippians 4:8, 9 (NAS)

I hope these verses serve as a source of encouragement to you as they do to me. There is a joy known only through the Christian life that is not experienced anywhere else. It is the joy of the Lord in your heart. It is a joy that does not fade away and grows deeper with each year of your Christian adventure. It is a strength that is ours no matter how tough things become. It is courage to live today and tomorrow for the love of Christ grows stronger in us as time goes by.

PROVISIONS

Provisions made for you and me, oh, yes! There are countless provisions made for those who want to live the abundant life of Christ and the provisions are ours for the claiming. We, who know Christ, have so very much going for us. We should rejoice in being a part of the abundant life. We have the opportunity to get outside of ourselves and serve the Lord as a vessel of love as we allow our faith to develop and grow.

It would be foolish of me to try to advise you concerning all of the things which the Lord can accomplish through you. You see, each of us has to allow our faith to grow and enlarge as the Lord opens the doors of life to us. As each door opens, we will achieve a purpose or set a special goal which will teach us more about His special love. With a teachable spirit, we will learn quickly the things which God wants to reveal to us. Through it all, our lives will become different, more Christ-like.

As faith develops, the work of the Lord Jesus Christ becomes more evident. We see Him working in all areas of life. As situations change and our spirits develop into a deeper understanding of God's nature we gain a deeper awareness of the glory of the Lord. The Christian who should develop a deeper faith will never have to stand back and say, "I wish that I had . . ." for they will have and they will be glad they did.

SUMMARY

This chapter has been a difficult one for me to share with you because it clearly defines our most important spiritual need for a fuller faith and deeper trust in Christ. You see, it is one thing for us to live with the knowledge of Christ, but quite another to live with Christ as a part of our daily routine. Our freedom, as Christians, allows us to choose the sort of Christian life we desire. Sometimes that choice is not easy to make.

For some of us there is no commitment to go beyond acceptance of Christ. For others there is the need to further develop and explore their faith. We can desire others to know just enough of Christ to get them by, or we can seek Him to become active in our daily routines and reveal Himself to us. We can allow our faith to blossom or we can allow the fruit to die on the vine. The choice is entirely up to us.

We are taught that we are to bear fruit. We are to gain insight and wisdom from the Lord and to share it. We are supposed to spread the "good news" around so others will know Christ. We are to give away more than we keep of our faith that the glory of the Lord might shine through for the world to see. We can be ever so much more than we are today, if only we will submit to the call of the Lord Jesus Christ. With our commitment of faith and trust we will reach out for the abundant life which allows Christ to be Number One. Our faith commitment will allow our spirits to share the love of Christ with a world that is in desperate need of love.

Questions

1. Why is the importance of a personal commitment to Christ necessary?

2. Why do we turn away from unpleasing areas of our life when we become God's person of commitment?

3. What are some of the things you need to give up so that your faith will grow and expand? Why?

4. Why should we "occupy our minds with thoughts of Christ?"

5. What exciting information do you find in Romans 8:38, 39?

6. Why do Christians tend to lose heart and fade away in their promises to Christ?

7. What happens when our faith begins to expand? Why?

8. What are some of the blessings learned as we place others first?

9. How is our faith measured?

10. Whose standards do we live by? (Be honest, don't fudge on this question.)

11. What are some of the provisions Christ has made for us?

12. How do these provisions affect our lifestyle?

13. Why should we give our faith away instead of hoarding it for ourselves?

14. What is the most important section of this chapter on being God's person of commitment to you as you study it?

7

Learning to say "I love you"

"I love you!" We've heard those words spoken to us, among us and around us. Sometimes the words are spoken in a half-hearted manner meaning little more than "I am deeply fond of you," but true love, the love of Christ means much more than this. Christ-like love is a love that radiates concern and fills others with concern for one another.

Many Christian men and women are unable to utter the words, "I love you," to another person. Perhaps there is a feeling of vulnerability or weakness when this person's expression of genuine concern is uttered verbally, or it may be that it is difficult to verbalize thoughts protected and shielded deeply within the heart. Whatever the reason we give for failure to express love, a genuine Christ-style love is a necessary part of life. Without love in our hearts, it is difficult for us to function as committed Christians.

The first time I told another Christian person, "I love you from my heart," I was rejected. This person did not understand what I was trying to say and misinterpreted my words. Perhaps she thought I had gone a bit crazy, or maybe she just wasn't willing to accept the Christ-like love; for whatever the reason, she began an open rejection of me. As a baby Christian, I did not understand that it was not my love she rejected but the love of God. She simply was not ready to accept God's love as it was offered by genuine love through Christ.

As time went on she separated herself from me more and more. Finally, there was no contact at all with her. This rejection caused a major setback in my Christian life and I soon found myself unable to make personal commitments to others because of this rejection. For well over a year I struggled with this problem and never found any comfort. The setback rendered my life inoperable in my Christian service.

I didn't like being vulnerable. Time and time again, I wished I had never uttered my expression of Christian love to this woman but I had, and that could never be changed. Resentment set in and I turned away from all my involvement in the church. "If this is the way Christians behave toward one another," I reasoned, "I'll have nothing to do with it."

For over three years my heart grew cold and bitter toward other Christians. I ignored contact with people in the church like they had the plague. I had not realized that too much of my life hinged on this one relationship. Although it had not been a successful relationship, it had been an important one. I learned from it that I cannot and should not hinge my relationship with Him on my personal friendship with another person. He taught me that it was He who should come first. My friendships with the friends I choose and my personal relationships need to be guided by Jesus' loving touch.

In time, Christ gave me a few distant relationships with other Christian people. I suppose they wondered why I was so standoffish, but I just couldn't help it. My fear was great!

I didn't want to be hurt. But God had another lesson prepared for me to learn concerning Christian love.

One day my spirit was moved to speak to a friend who was struggling with some serious problems. "Did you know that I really do love you with the love of the Lord?" I asked. A gentle smile crossed her face as she replied, "Yes, I do but I can't return that love to you. You see," she said, "I don't love you in the same way and I never will. I want a different kind of life than what you have and you and I can never be close."

Again, I felt as though I had been slapped in the face. Frustration and hurt set in and took firm hold of my spirit. I wondered what it was that caused people to react to me in such a manner. Am I so unlovable? What's wrong with me? Why does this keep happening to me? How could I allow myself to fall into this trap again?

Finally, in total and complete exasperation and with a deeply wounded spirit I found counsel for my problem. "Why doesn't anybody love me? What is it that causes this rejection in people?" I asked.

The answers helped me find the explanation I so desperately needed. "Perhaps," said my friend in a quiet voice, "you want the wrong people to love you for the wrong reasons. You are deeply loved by several people. And your problem, Frances, is that you want to pick and choose the people you love. You want to be loved by people who simply don't know how to love like Christ loved. You can't make people love you just because you love them. There are many people who are unwilling to love anyone because it takes a commitment to love with the love of Christ. And most people aren't willing to make that kind of commitment."

I considered this conversation for a long while. As I prayed and asked the Lord to show me how to overcome this problem and my heartaches, He opened my heart to gain a new understanding of Christian love. Please read on so that you may discover what I learned about love:

- Some people have almost no feelings at all for anyone. Their lives revolve around themselves and they really feel they don't need to be loved by anyone outside of their families.

- There are people who have limited compassion for others. Just because I feel compassionate doesn't mean everyone else is.

- Many people have wrong priorities. They just aren't concerned with anyone's needs but their own. They simply have us tuned out.

- Some people have decided they have no need for Christ-like love. They have hearts that are turned in another direction and anything to do with the Lord turns them off. They ignore love because they are seeking to ignore Christ.

- More than likely the persons who have so deeply hurt my spirit don't even know it. They have no attachments for me because they simply have no room in their heart for me. It may be that we do not have a like spirit but a distant spirit.

- Many people are unwilling to receive Christian love because they don't want Christ to grip their heart and change their spirit. They may like the way they live, and to submit their present nature to Christ's nature would mean change is necessary. A few of these people are caught between two worlds, the spiritual and the natural.

With these understandings, I have begun to acknowledge that not everyone is going to like me, let alone love me. It may be that these people will never change but then again who knows. I must live with the thought that in giving out love, I must expect nothing in return. Christ will supply the responses and the results as He sees fit, not as I desire things to be.

As a committed Christian our spirit changes and our past relationships with others may need altering. With a deeper understanding of Christ we experience more of the Holy Spirit than the nominal believer experiences. Our lives are open channels, sensitive and submissive to the voice of the Holy Spirit as it speaks to our spirit. The Spirit allows us to learn, as we share our love, that we have different relationships and feelings toward each person we know.

If we truly want to love others, as Christ taught us to love, we will have to become alienated from the unlovely spirit that seeks to convince us we have nothing to offer anyone. We must continue to love through thick and thin. Love never gives up. The wonderful thing about Christian love is that you can continue giving it away and never run short of it. Even in loving someone who is less concerned for you, there is an abundance of love you can offer them. We can love, with the love of Christ, and not carry the unnecessary burden of, "Will they love me in return?" We just let Christ function through us and He will handle each individual relationship as He desires.

Love makes us approachable. Now think for a minute, how many people do you really know as approachable? Not many. Most of us find it uncomfortable to be approached, but Christian love is open, available, and ready to touch the lives of others as Christ leads the way. *All* of us are supposed to exercise this love and allow the Spirit to fill our lives with more of it every day we live. When I wrote my first book, *A Book of Devotions for Today's Woman,* I was scared that my expression of love and concern for others would make me too vulnerable. But instead what I have found is that people are more considerate and loving toward me. When others view their lives with struggles, heartaches, vulnerable weaknesses, and the need for love, something happens. Love springs forth and opens up within us as we see someone else experience many of the same things we encounter. We view this person not as "someone who's got it made" but as someone who is trying to live for Christ just as we are.

Love makes our lives more open and available. One lady made me laugh one afternoon when I was shopping in a local store. She smiled broadly and said, "I know you. *Golly, do I know you!* I've read two of your books and I know your heart inside and out, and you know what, you're a lot like me." We laughed at her words but the truth is, there are a lot of people like me, like you, who seek to share their love in some manner with all people. When we see love reflected in another person's life we find it is difficult to ignore them. The love of Christ should draw us to one another for support, encouragement, fellowship, and godly love.

Love should build confidence. In learning how to share my love the Lord showed me that I need not feel uncertain or insecure concerning other's views. After all He *has promised* to supply my needs according to His riches. I have nothing to fear in sharing love and neither do you for the perfect love of Christ is a builder not a destroyer. Those who refuse or neglect to accept our love might damage us a bit, but our spirits will only grow stronger in the Lord's love.

Christian love causes spiritual maturity to develop and expand. In our expression of Christian love we cannot help but seek a closer relationship to Christ. The more knowledge and wisdom we gain concerning love relationships in the family of God, the more we will want to share this love. We grow deeper in love with Christ as we submit our lives to Him and allow His complete love to flow freely through our hearts. The person who is unloving and distant is not a maturing Christian, for love is a vital part of the Christian walk. Many Christians can recite memorized Scriptures and tell you that without Christ, there is nothing much to live for. They have a set plan of witness, but unless that witness shows love their plan leaves something to be desired. Unless they allow the love of Christ to be top priority in their lives they just tend to make a great deal of noise. Read 1 Corinthians 13 for a full description of how God desires love to function and what love is to do in the life of a believer.

Christian love is not a possessive love. It does not give with expectation of getting something in return. This love tells another, "You are important to the Lord Jesus Christ. I am concerned for you as Christ is concerned. I love you with no strings attached and desire that you know this love. My love for you is a love given from God knowing that you are valued by God. My love is available to you in a spirit of concern." Sometimes this kind of love is not understood by another person and if this happens to you don't be overly concerned about it. Maybe the Lord is preparing the way for this person's heart to be opened to the Word of God. Whatever you experience now, this person, even if they pretend to ignore you, has been touched by the Spirit of the Living Lord through your expression of love.

Our love is expressed in a variety of ways: A phone call, a card, a simple greeting at the grocery store, a note to say, "I'm thinking of you," a touching of hands, a pat on the back, or even a simple look can express love to another. Love, Christ-like love, provides the giver and the receiver a united opportunity to change their hearts and make free choices that lead to greater understanding of their faith. Actually, it is impossible for us to humanly judge the impact love makes on the life of another.

Love always seeks to make the other person feel glad and at peace. Consider Paul's words, "Therefore if there is any consolation in Christ, if any comfort of love, if any fellowship of the Spirit, if any affection and mercy, fulfill my joy by being like-minded, having the same love being of one accord, of one mind. Let nothing be done, through selfish ambition, or conceit, but in lowliness of mind, let each esteem another better than himself. Let each of you look out not only for his own interests, but also for the interests of others. Let this mind be in you which was also in Christ Jesus." Philippians 2:1–5 (NKJV)

Christian love does not look to its own interest first but to the interests of others. This love is humble and compassionate. It is not concerned with empty conceit or self-seeking egos. It has discovered that happiness is found in the encouraging love we share with another person through the Spirit of God.

I can almost hear some of you say, "But how can I consider someone else more important than myself? After all I have so many needs and my heart aches with the desire to be cared for." Since I have been in this position at one time or another in my life then allow me to share with you some of the lessons I have learned. Although my needs and desires still exist, the Lord has showed me something important concerning life. We all consider our burdens heavy and our needs unsurmountable at times. At this point, we acknowledge our need for help. And when I begin to look outside of my own burdens, my own needs, my own desires and wants, something happens within my spirit. I begin to really look at other people and what's happening in their lives. I want to be their Christian friend and establish a relationship based on the love of Jesus.

The more I focus in on helping someone, sharing their burden, praying for them, the less concerned I become for my needs. Learning to put others first allows us to free ourselves from the emotional torture that pulls our spirits apart. As my sensitive spirit reaches out to become part of another person's life for a few moments then my needs are set aside. The less I consider myself, the more love I am able to share, for my love no longer centers around myself but is offered in genuine concern for another. And, as I am often reminded, God's promises become stronger and mean more to me when I share my loving nature. It's strange, but the promises of God seem to strengthen me as I see the Lord work in the life of another. The storms are quieted when I view the Lord's handiwork in someone else's life. The Spirit of the Lord gives security and confidence to me telling me that my needs will be met. These needs are met, in due time.

"The one who loves his brother abides in the light and there is no cause for stumbling in him." 1 John 2:10 (NAS) Practicing Christ-like love provides us with the opportunity to avoid stumbling over the spiritual obstacles set in our path. Instead of stumbling over personal weaknesses, I learn to view them as they are, evaluate them, and walk around them. Because the love of Christ sheds light in my life, I can even leap over these obstacles (spiritually speaking of course) and be on my way because I view obstacles and pitfalls as they are. They are open to my view and I won't stumble into danger because I cannot see what is happening all around me. Through the sharing of His love I see my own needs in a different light, His light.

Let's make sure that this isn't confusing to some of you. It is too important to overlook or misunderstand in the spiritual context it is written. Christ's light, in me and in you, sheds light in all areas of our lives. The closer our relationship with the Lord the more light is ours. The more we view His promises as secure and unshakable the more confident we grow in our beliefs, knowing all along that the One in whom we believe is the Almighty God. The Spirit truly opens our eyes to God's goodness. It allows us to give full consideration to God's love as we share that love with others. As we share God's love and allow His Spirit to touch the hearts of others, through us, then we are truly blessed.

One of the blessings as taught in verse 10 of 1 John 2 is that the light (His light) will help us view matters in a different perspective than before. While we may be concerned with some areas of our life, we can have full confidence that the Lord will provide the answers and the solutions to the problems we encounter. That truth assures our hearts and lifts our spirits as followers of Christ. Perfect love, His love, protects, guides, heals, and provides for our real needs. Because we have His love we are to share it with all people and as we do our lives are deeply enriched with unspeakable joy.

THE DEPTH OF OUR LOVE COMMITMENT

Christ-like love is visible to those who open their eyes to it. It comes in various forms because each Christian has his own unique gift of love to offer. With our promise we gain many new spiritual insights concerning our faith and our belief in Christ; and along with this we gain spiritual knowledge that love has no strings attached.

As we consider Christ-like love, we should consider some of the teachings concerning love:

- "We love because He first loved us." 1 John 4:19 (NAS)

- "By this we know love, because He laid down His life for us. And we ought to lay down our lives for the brethren. But whoever has this world's goods, and sees his brother in need, and shuts up his heart from him, how does the love of God dwell in him? My little children, let us not love in word or in tongue, but in deed and in truth. And by this we know that we are of the truth, and shall assure our hearts before Him." 1 John 3:16–19 (NKJV)

- "Beloved, let us love one another, for love is of God; and everyone who loves is born of God and knows God. He who does not love does not know God, for God is love." 1 John 4:7, 8 (NAS)

- "Whoever confesses that Jesus is the Son of God, God dwells in him, and he in God. And we have known and believed the love that God has for us. God is love, and he who dwells in love dwells in God, and God in him." 1 John 4:15–17 (NKJV)

- "Whoever believes that Jesus is the Christ is born of God; and whoever loves the Father loves the child born of Him. By this we know that we love the children of God, when we love God and observe His commandments. For this is the love of God, that we keep His commandments; and His commandments are not burdensome." 1 John 5:1–3 (NAS)

The verses of Scripture go on and on teaching us the truths of God. It is necessary for us to understand these thoughts, relate to them, and apply them to situations in our lives each day. God demonstrates His love through you and me. He displays the truth and accuracy of His promises through our commitment of faith. Our promise to follow Jesus is a lifelong part of our faith and should be considered with a sincere heart.

As we understand the concept of Christian love, we will desire to share it. Love provides opportunities for improvement in our lives. We can be Spirit-filled people who seek to keep their vows to God who fills our lives with challenging opportunities to live life to the fullest, His way. Love improves. Love builds up. Love encourages. Love gives hope. Love fills our souls with a promise that is not erased in time and recalls the truth that "He first loved us." That's exciting!

As I sit and type these words, my heart feels there is a special need to express some very real concerns I hold about the obligations we have to love each other. My challenge to you is this:

- Search your hearts to determine how love flows in your life.

- Consider those you have not or will not love for one reason or another. Why won't you? How do you think the Lord considers this reasoning?

- Decide to communicate Christ-like love to someone who has not been impressive to your nature. Begin to pray for them and ask God why this person is so unlovable to you. Pray for this person each day and see if there is some manner in which our Lord will use your life to touch their spirit. *Be open to the Holy Spirit within you.*

- Restore a love commitment you have allowed to fade away. There is someone in your life who waits to have a word of encouragement and love from you. This person may be a former friend, someone you have worked with, someone with whom you have had words and expressed bitterness, a family member, or a member of the church family. Restore a loving relationship with that person as soon as possible.

- Determine in your heart whether your promises are valid or not. Do you really intend to be a godly person or are you merely playing a game? Do you really want to reach out and be the person He wants you to be, or will you continue to hold out on God? Determine in your mind and heart what standards you seek to follow, and ask the Lord to open doors of opportunity to you to serve as a vessel of love and concern.

- Be approachable. Remember that we all need someone and a Christian friend is a rare gift. Be approachable and allow the love of Christ to flow openly and freely so that others might receive a blessing from your life.

- Be confident. Know that the Lord keeps His promises and because you *know* and *believe* in Him there is an unbreakable bond of love between you. Christian, rejoice and be filled with His Spirit and allow His Spirit to give your life new and deeper meaning.

We need not be spiritual nomads drifting from place to place. But we are called to be Children of God, walking in the light and sharing our lives as Christ provides us opportunities. The love offered us, through the Spirit, is to expand and enlarge as we share our spirit of love with those we meet. Christian, the challenge is great. There is *no greater challenge in this life* than to be a spirit-filled, godly person who shares a loving spirit wherever the Lord tells him to plant a seed. It is my hope that you will discover the blessing of learning to say, "I love you," for in those blessings are some of life's happiest moments.

Questions

1. Why is it so difficult to say to someone, "I love you"?

2. Why are many people unwilling to utter these words?

3. Is it important for Christians to openly express love to one another? Why?

4. How does the Lord use our expression of love in the life of the unbeliever to change his life?

5. What are some of the characteristics of the person who is unwilling or denies the opportunity to love others?

6. What are some of the strong qualities of Christ-like love?

7. What one person, in your life, has avoided your love and why?

8. Do you think the love Christians express is understood by the majority of persons? Express your answer fully in your notebook.

9. Does being vulnerable bother you?

10. How should we view our opportunities to share the love of Christ that we feel in our hearts?

11. Why are many men and women unwilling to make a commitment of Christian love to another person?

12. How do we serve as vessels of love for Christ?

13. How important is it that we maintain a sensitive spirit as we journey the road of life?

14. Why should we be available to share Christ-like love with those we consider unlovable?

15. Consider one or two people that you have more or less ignored because their spirit seemed to clash with yours? Is there something within your spirit that tells you that you need to change your attitudes toward this person? Why or why not?

16. Locate three verses from the Scripture which teach you something important about love. Write them in your notebook and then read them out loud. When you have done this, spend some time really considering what these Scriptures are teaching you. What have you learned from them?

17. What verses in this chapter have stood out as important truths concerning love and your relationship with the Lord at this stage in your life?

18. What areas of your life need some altering so that the full love of Christ can flow through you?

8

Considering some who have made promises or commitments

The results of a working faith are seen when we begin to accomplish something valid and useful in our lives. This is called bearing fruit. This chapter is dedicated to those men and women who have made a commitment to carry through with their promises and commitments. As I have considered these persons, the promises and the results learned in trusting our Lord, I have come up with a list of men and women whom we should consider as having made a commitment to the Lord.

Although my list might contain such greats as Moses, Joseph, Peter, and John, I have decided not to concentrate my efforts on them at this point, but to look at some lesser known Bible personalities. It is my hope that considering those who have gone before us, you will gain a new interest in learning more about their lives.

While Paul symbolizes the main crusader to the Gentiles, we should not and cannot overlook Barnabas. Barnabas was a man who was an encourager, an enlightener, a supporter of the "good news" of Jesus Christ as it was carried forth by those who shared the fellowship of the early church.

Barnabas was more than Paul's faithful sidekick, he was a vessel of service, a caring member of the body of Christ, as he served as an encourager and uplifter to those near him. We quickly learn as we read in Acts Chapters 9–14 a great deal of information concerning Barnabas. He was a truly dedicated Christian. He believed in Christ and made a personal commitment to Him. With this personal commitment, there was a deep degree of sensitivity and willingness to submit his life to the calling of the Holy Spirit. When Paul was converted the believers were terribly afraid of him. They were skeptical and wondered if Paul's conversion was a clever trick or a true life-changing experience. After all, Paul's reputation was awesome and he was deeply feared.

The Holy Spirit quickly sent Barnabas to befriend Paul. Barnabas talked with Paul and listened as the new convert shared his conversion experience on the road to Damascus. Barnabas realized Paul was sincere in his commitment to Christ. But the facts remained that Paul was present at the stoning of Stephen, and he had promised to do everything within his power to rid the world of these followers of Jesus. Barnabas knew Paul desired acceptance by the followers of Jesus, but his reputation made that almost impossible. Barnabas wondered what one man could do to change the minds of so many, and yet he was willing to speak out for Paul because the Holy Spirit instructed him to do so. Were it not for Barnabas' sensitivity and caring spirit, Paul's ministry would have suffered a tremendous setback. But

Barnabas the encourager, the friend, the helper, came through for Paul.

When Barnabas spoke on Paul's behalf the people listened with intensity. They were interested in what he said and since he was highly respected, the people believed and accepted Paul as one of them. His commitment to the Lord had just begun as the Holy Spirit commissioned these men to travel together as missionaries and journey to Antioch. Barnabas was with Paul as they worked jointly to establish the first churches in the region. He stood firm and dedicated to serving the Lord as he traveled throughout the region, and no doubt Paul was glad to have him along on the first missionary journey to the Gentiles.

Paul regarded Barnabas as a faithful worker, a dedicated man, and a trusted friend. Paul and Barnabas carried the message of Jesus Christ across the land to all who listened and desired to learn about Christ. Barnabas was a man filled with trust in the Lord. He worked faithfully and kept his promises to serve the Lord wherever the Lord sent him.

When I consider Barnabas, a dear Christian brother comes to mind, Roy Buckelew. Roy served as our interim pastor for several months as we waited for a new pastor for our church. One Sunday morning Roy said, "I like to think of myself as a man like Barnabas. I am an encourager. I am a helper. You can all call me 'Barnabas Buckelew.' I want to be your friend and helper while I serve as interim pastor of this church."

We all laughed when Roy called himself Barnabas, but we weren't laughing over the rest of his statement. In fact, I learned first hand how much of an encourager Roy could be. Roy counseled with me one day when I was really spiritually down. He expressed joy and happiness as I shared some of my writing ideas with him. He built me up in Christian love and displayed that Christ-like concern that all Christians need to have for each other. Roy Buckelew has earned a place in my heart as my special encourager in a time when I made some important decisions concerning my writing career.

Roy wrote me two encouraging notes as he read my materials. He said he was happy for me and he felt sure that our Lord would use my words to touch lives. Roy Buckelew's words touched my spirit and I began to gain a new confidence in what the Lord was leading me to do. Through Roy's life I found that we all need to have encouragers.

Roy listened once again as I told him about my personal fears concerning public speaking. Roy, a professor of speech, a minister in the church, a friend, an encourager, told me this, "Frances, in time, the Lord will take away that fear and replace it with something unshakable. The Lord will teach you when you speak to say things that you would want to hear if you were listening to someone else speak." Roy's words encouraged me beyond any words ever spoken to me. My Barnabas told me, "From the things that I have read, I am sure the Lord's going to use your talents; just be yourself and let Christ work through your life to reach others."

My Barnabas helped me to understand my struggle in a different way. As a Christian encourager, he allowed me to see my potential for Christian service. I am glad to have touched lives with Roy because I learned some important facts from him. And you know what? I feel just a bit wiser having known a Barnabas in my Christian life.

Knowing a Barnabas and calling him or her your Christian friend is one of the blessings of the Christian life. We all need to be aware of one another's needs and burdens, and when we become a Barnabas we can surely lighten the burdens that many Christians bear. Each Christian needs at least one Barnabas in their life. The person with the Barnabas personality is strong in the Lord, sensitive in spirit, and filled with a Christ-like love. While these qualities are very rare and few of us seek to be a Barnabas, we all need to strive to be a bit like Barnabas. And if you are called to be a Barnabas remember this, your encouragement gives hope in times of discouragement and despair.

Perhaps you are facing some moments of despair and need your own personal words of encouragement. If you do, please let me be your personal Barnabas, right now, at this moment.

I know your life is of great worth to the living Lord. I know you have needs and heartaches. Perhaps you feel no one truly understands your heart or your feelings; well, our Lord does. Our Lord is truly concerned that you know and experience the Christian life to the fullest, and He wants you to know that He loves you a great deal.

The Lord would have you to know, Christian, that the things you think, the way you react, and the things you work for and do as a Christian soldier are not unnoticed by Him. He wants you to realize that all that you do is not done in vain when you dedicate your efforts to Him. Be of good courage and stand firm. Look forward to sharing your life with others with the confidence of knowing that He created you as a special person with a specific purpose. Make your own personal promise to Christ to follow after Him. Reach out and experience life, in Christ, with joy and peace. Allow Christ to present Himself to you and to challenge your heart this very day.

If at anytime you need a Barnabas, an encourager, an uplifter, here I am. I am willing to share whatever words the Lord will give me on your behalf to encourage you. You don't have to be without a personal encourager, and if you really want one, here I am. If you want to write me, mail your letter to:

Mrs. Frances Carroll
P.O. Box 1537
Russellville, Arkansas 72801

2 Kings 21–23 relates the story of this young king. To gain a little background on him, let me recap the story for you. Then you will understand why his personal commitment to the Lord was important.

Evil had ruled in the land of Israel for a very long while. King Manasseh had reigned 55 years. He was a really evil king. In fact, he was so evil that many of the deeds he was responsible for were never recorded in the chronicles of Kings.

Manasseh was such a rotten fellow that he encouraged his own sons to learn and practice witchcraft. He was also involved with mediums and spirits. We know that this sort of thing is evil and our Lord does not honor such practices. But that didn't seem to bother Manasseh. In truth, he really didn't care what the Lord thought for he worshipped Baal and other idols. Sun worship and all sorts of things were practiced in the kingdom and among the people. The people, themselves, had become corrupt and had turned away from God. (That is, almost all of them had.)

Well, the Scriptures tell us that Manasseh had a lot of innocent blood shed for no reason at all. He was a rotten egg. When Manasseh died, his son Amon became King. Amon wasn't any better than his dad. The Scriptures tell us that he practiced the same sort of deeds and worshipped the same idols.

I guess the people were beginning to get a little tired of all of this, as some of them plotted against Amon and killed him. The people who plotted against Amon were also conspired against and removed. These people made Josiah, Amon's son, king. The boy was a mere eight years old.

The Bible says, "He did what was right in the sight of the Lord. His course was true and certain." What a relief that must have been to some of the people.

At any rate, Josiah sent a man to the house of the Lord to restore it. He told this man to have the workmen, builders, and stone-masons to do whatever was necessary to restore it. He advised the man not to keep an account of their expenses for they were faithful and trustworthy. The house of the Lord was rebuilt by these dedicated people and I feel certain our Lord was truly pleased with Josiah.

The high priest, Helkiah, brought to Shaphran, the scribe, a book of the Law that was found within the house of the Lord. After the scribe read it he took the book to the king.

The king was deeply disturbed as the scribe read the contents of the book to him. He realized how evil and deceptive the people had been as they worshipped false idols, sought after mediums, and listened to the counsel of spirits. He wondered why God had not yet acted to destroy or punish the people, no doubt, and felt that God must be very angry with all the people.

Josiah knew his father and his father before him had often ignored God. They had not listened wisely and sought God but pursued evil desires and a lustful way of life. In the 23rd chapter of 2 Kings we learn that Josiah makes a covenant (a promise) to the Lord. In this promise he "sought to walk after the Lord and keep His commandments and statutes. I will," he stated in his vow, "with all my heart and soul obey the words of the covenant written in this book." All of the people joined with Josiah in making the covenant.

Some of the changes which came because of Josiah's commitment to the Lord were:

- Reinstitution of the Passover Feast
- Burning of the vessels of Baal
- Doing away with the idolatrous priests
- Removal of mediums, spiritists, and idols in the land of Judah and in Jerusalem
- Burning of the chariots of the sungod
- Doing away with the horses given to the sungod

- The houses of the male cult prostitutes were broken down
- Burning and scattering of the ashes of the idols

The Scriptures have some very interesting words concerning King Josiah, "And before him there was no king like him who turned to the Lord with all his heart and with all his soul and with all his might, according to all the laws of Moses; nor did any like him arise after him." (NAS) verses 23–25

We must not overlook the importance of this king's contribution to the world of that day. When things looked hopeless and there was little godliness among the people, Josiah rose up to lead them. As a young man he realized the necessity of restoring good to the kingdom of Israel. It took courage and wisdom to understand that God will not let man go without punishment for wickedness and evil.

No doubt the things he did brought reform within the country. The evil no longer dominated the actions of the people. Josiah wanted his people to be spared the punishment of God, and although God did punish the people they were given another chance to seek Him.

GIDEON

Hebrews 11:32 describes Gideon as a man of faith. Gideon's commitment to the Lord is found in Judges 6–8. This Old Testament story is a strange one. We will not go into all the little details, but the story is worth the fifteen minutes you will spend reading it. Read it and see what happened to Gideon.

Gideon was called by God to deliver Israel from Midianite domination. An angel first came and spoke to Gideon as he was beating out wheat to hide it from the Midianites. I expect it was quite an experience as Gideon questioned the angel after the angel announced, "The Lord is with you, O valiant warrior."

Gideon asked, "If the Lord is with us, why then has all this happened to us?" The angel's response was "Go in this your strength and deliver Israel from the hand of Midian. Have I not sent you?" Later that night the same angel came to him again and told him to destroy his father's shrine of Baal. The Bible tells us the Spirit of the Lord came upon Gideon. Gideon received a challenge of a lifetime and responded to the call of God. He could have ignored the call but he did not. He made a promise to be God's man, and promised to see the task through, thus allowing the Spirit of the Lord to flow through him.

Read how Gideon gathered his unique army of 300 men. It is a story that will allow you to see God at work throughout this battle. Gideon kept his promises and remained faithful. His men were obedient to him and he was obedient to God. True commitment takes obedience to God's Spirit. When the timing was right Gideon and his army were victorious.

LUKE

As I view my notes and prepare to discuss Luke with you there is a feeling of love and admiration for him deep within my heart. It would be good for us to recall Luke as an important member of the early Christian community as well as a respected physician.

Luke was a good friend of Paul's and is mentioned in his writings. Although we are not concentrating on Paul, we should remain aware that Luke's commitment to Paul, in the name of Christ, was unshakable. Luke was not a man who demanded the out-front attention, but was fully capable of serving wherever the Lord led him.

Luke was a very spiritual man. He wrote the book of Luke in a manner which is not only real but accurate and exciting to read. As a physician, Luke was accustomed to details and through his writings we learn some of the details that the other writers of the gospel bypassed.

Luke was a truly committed man of God. He, like many others, had made a full commitment to follow Christ and serve as a vessel of love and service. He was tremendously sensitive in nature and very attentive to the people and events surrounding him. He stressed the fulfillment of the Old Testament prophecies concerning the life of Jesus as he wrote the book of Luke. Luke was a hard worker and a dedicated man of God.

When we consider Doctor Luke's promises to our Lord and his commitment as an apostle, we might want to refresh our memories of the book of Luke. Within each chapter we learn something important. It is Luke who told us the full story of John the Baptist: the facts concerning the conception of Jesus: an indepth look at the prayers of Jesus, and; who makes a skillful attempt to trace the ancestry of Jesus back to Adam.

We should be more than a little thankful for the commitment of Luke to his work. You see, Christian, he did not just tell those about him the "good news" but he shared it with you and me. He was an encourager used to tell us the truth of God concerning Jesus Christ. We owe a tremendous debt to our brother in Christ, Luke, for he pursued his commitment to Christ so that generations which were to follow would have an indepth look at Christ.

JOSEPH OF ARIMATHEA

How could a member of the Sanhedrin (council) have a commitment to our Lord? After all they were in part responsible for his death. I expect Joseph was fully committed to Christ and that he suffered deeply as he watched Jesus die on the cross at Calvary.

Joseph had become a secret disciple of Christ. He had to be quiet and discreet about his belief because he was fearful of what might happen to him. It wasn't the acceptable thing to do, after all, to believe in and accept this man Jesus as the Messiah. But Joseph did believe. He did trust. He did accept the gift of salvation through Christ and was committed to Christ.

Joseph's commitment to Christ came at a most important moment in history. It was Joseph who went to Pilate and requested the body of Christ that it might be tended to for burial. Perhaps we don't fully understand the impact of Joseph's commitment as he openly demonstrated his faith by tending to the last earthly needs of the Savior's lifeless body. Pilate was aware of this man's reputation as a leader in the community, so Pilate agreed to turn over Jesus' body to him for burial.

Joseph watched and grieved as Christ's body was taken from the cross. What an experience it must have been for him. Joseph saw to it that our Lord's body was wrapped in new linen and anointed with precious spices for burial. I expect he wept as the burial cloth was placed over the face of Jesus. When everything had been tended to and it was time to leave, the tomb was sealed. He did not want anyone to steal away the body of the Lord. Joseph's commitment to Christ left nothing undone. He did everything completely and oversaw the tasks at hand.

There is no doubt in my mind that the Lord used Joseph as a servant of Christ from that day on. I expect he made it clear that his commitment was to Christ and not to mankind. Joseph followed through and did not neglect the burial of our Lord's body. The tomb in which the body was laid had been purchased for his own burial, but considering the Lord's needs for a temporary resting place, he gave this new tomb as a resting place for our Lord. What blessings he must have received because his commitment to Christ stood firm and strong.

APOLLOS

One of my favorite people in the New Testament era is Apollos. He was a follower of John the Baptist. He did not have full knowledge of the Lord's message but spoke with fervor with the facts he had.

Apollos and his twelve companions traveled about speaking to the people. Their message, as was John the Baptist's, was "Repent for the kingdom of heaven is at hand." A badly needed message that few felt the commitment to share.

Aquila and Priscilla, two strong-hearted Christians, heard his message and quickly realized he needed to be given the complete facts concerning Jesus. They realized what a powerful speaker this man was and knew that when he understood the full truth concerning Christ his commitment would grow deeper and stronger.

What a joy it must have been for Apollos when two mature Christians approached him. They shared their knowledge of Christ giving him all the information they knew concerning Jesus Christ as Lord and Savior of mankind. Imagine what an impact that made on his speaking. New enthusiasm filled his heart. Apollos with an encouraged heart and a renewed spirit could now share all the facts concerning his faith in Christ.

There are many more examples of commitment we could cite in this chapter. The list is endless. Consider the men and women you know who have made promises to Christ and see Christ as a moving force in their lives. The life that is committed to Christ is never the same again. The mundane Christian life is set aside because the committed Christian is eager to step into new adventure and experience a life that has much more meaning than ever before. Each life represented in this chapter has made a different impact and contribution through their experiences in following God. Now that we have reached the end of this chapter we must view our individual lives and ask ourselves, are we fully committed to Christ? If not, why not? Our next chapter talks about the steps to commitment in the Christian life. Let us prepare our minds and hearts for that lesson of truth.

Questions

1. What qualities stand out, in your mind, concerning Barnabas' commitment to Christ?

2. How does an encouraging spirit help another person as they go through life?

3. Why do you think Josiah was so convinced he needed to change the nation's evil habits?

4. When you consider what this chapter has to say concerning mediums, spirits, and evil practices, why do you think those are things Josiah said had to be done away with?

5. What does it mean, "He did right in the eyes of the Lord"?

6. How should a commitment to the Lord be made?

7. Read the story of Gideon. How did he test God to make sure the instruction he received was from God?

8. Why do you think he did this?

9. How can the Spirit of the Lord flow through you and me?

10. Why would we want it to?

11. Consider Joseph of Arimathea. Do you think his commitment to the Lord, as a secret believer, was effective? What do you think the people might have thought when Joseph claimed Christ's body for burial?

12. Do you think Joseph made an impact on the followers of Jesus through his actions and deeds? Why or why not?

9

Steps to take toward commitment

My children play a game I played as a child called "May I." The object of this game is to make a series of moves, using "baby steps, giant steps, etc." to complete a course and cross the finish line first. The only drawback in the game occurs if the judge likes one person more than another. If you happen to be the one liked most, you can be fairly sure of winning but the one considered least comes up short.

With our Christian commitment we take steps to reach the finish line and run our own personal race. The only difference is that this is not a game. Our judge is not partial, because God treats all of us equally and judges us in the same manner. God wants all of us to finish as winners.

When we see other Christians and how they run their course we tend to feel they may have finished ahead of us. We think they have something that we don't have and that somehow God might have shortchanged us. Really, what has happened is this— throughout our lives we have chosen not to make decisions that would allow us to run the course of commitment with intensity. We have lagged behind allowing others to run ahead of us. We may have said "no" when we should have replied "yes" and our race is slowed to a casual walk.

Commitment to Christ is made on a daily basis. Steps toward commitment aren't taken by deciding to take step one and avoiding steps two and three and picking up again at step four. Each step toward commitment is of equal importance. With each step taken, we learn that we must be willing to walk with Christ and trust Him in "all things." And, as you might expect, some steps of commitment are easier to take than others because some of them cause us to change some of the unlovely areas of our lives that we might not want to give up. But through our total commitment to Christ we will find that nothing that is really important will be missing by being a complete person in Christ. And as we finish life's course and glance back over our lives, we are glad we stepped out with Jesus to gain the treasures He has for us.

Please allow me to share a personal thought with you concerning my promises and commitment toward the Lord. I use to wonder why some Christians seemed to have more of a Christ-like life than I had. I wanted what they had but I didn't know it came through an ever increasing commitment to Christ. I just didn't understand the blessings of walking closely with Christ. It seemed to me that the Christ-led woman looked like she had her life altogether and I knew my life was just the opposite.

You see, the aimless lifestyle many of us live is not necessary at all. We wander around in a spiritual maze seeking a course to travel and always taking a detour. But with the understanding that the abundant life is available to all of us, we need not walk through life without aims and goals. Once I decided I was through with spiritual detours and made my personal commitment to Christ, then my life discovered new meaning. Of course, we will all still get detoured from time to time. But as our commitment increases our detours decrease.

Commitment is:
- A state of being obligated to someone, something or a cause.
- A promise to follow through to the end.
- Saying, "Yes, I will. You can count on me."
- Being faithful to your word.
- Being stable and steadfast in deed and action.
- Being ready
- Being willing
- Being open and available
- Being submissive in nature

Commitment is so much more than meets the eye. Christian commitment is a way of life that says you are not living for yourself but for Christ. Commitment to Christ makes us certain and sure of ourselves because we allow the Holy Spirit to function freely through us, and through Him our doubts and fear are overcome.

PRESENT YOUR
LIFE TO CHRIST

"Here I am Lord, do with me whatever you will to enrich and bless my life and the life of others." Your promise to do or be whatever the Lord wants you to be is an exciting adventure. For with your promise to be whoever the Lord wants you to be the doors of faith open for you. You view the full light of Christ, and the warmth of Christ fills your heart as you draw into a closer relationship with Him.

Our thoughts need not be centered around fretting and fears about tomorrow for the peace of God begins to fill our souls. We begin to discover that it was not the "old self" who was important in our journey of faith but it is the "new me," regenerated and made alive by the power of Christ that has given us a life filled with purpose and meaning. Through our promise to follow Christ, His Spirit will begin to function with ease to create a better spirit within us. The "new me" gains stability and a new personality which functions not in selfishness but in submissiveness to the Lord. That is a blessing to the life of any believer.

SUBMISSIVENESS

Because I don't think most of us understand the term submissiveness, and our old nature tells us we don't want to submit to anyone or anything, I think we need to take a few minutes and talk it over. That old devil, the one who tries to mislead and misdirect our actions, often tells us that if we commit our lives fully to the Lord then we are little more than robots. Nothing could be further from the truth. Submissiveness to Christ is a willing change of attitude and heart.

Look at your life as it is right this minute. Are you 100% happy and pleased with it? Of course not! And you never will be content until you surrender those unlovely areas of life. All of us have secrets hidden away in our lives, things we need to get rid of which we know are not healthy or good for our lives. Well, through submission to Christ, simply saying, "Whatever I have is yours, Jesus, I even give you the garbage, the rotten stuff that's going bad, and I'll let you deal with it," the Lord begins to clean your spiritual house. He will rid our lives of those things which are unacceptable (garbage) and rid our lives of that rotten smell of wrongness and sinfulness caused by misdirection and disobedience. You see, Christ takes all of us as we are and cleans us up. He takes us out of Satan's spiritual dumpster, washes us with His precious blood, the blood that cleansed us from our own sinfulness at the cross of Calvary, and anoints us with His Spirit. He washes the germs of hate, despair, fear, envy, selfishness, deceitfulness, and all the other unloveliness away and replaces them with a new desire to be more like Jesus. In submissiveness to Christ we gain freedom to be the person we should be, Christ's person.

- Romans 12:1, 2 (NAS), "I urge you therefore, brethren, by the mercies of God, to present your bodies a living and holy sacrifice, acceptable to God, which is your spiritual service of worship. And do not be conformed to this world, but be transformed by the *renewing of your mind*, that you may prove what the will of God is, that which is good and acceptable and perfect."
Paul's words give us a firm foundation to build upon. To help us understand what our promises to Christ mean, let us discover the information Paul has provided us with:

- "Present your bodies"—our bodies are our housing while here on earth. As we live our lives, in the body, we are to "give" our bodies to Christ as an offering. Where the body goes the rest of our being follows, for our bodies are temporary storehouses for our spirit.
When you "present" yourself to God you are to be God's person. God takes you as you are and begins to prepare you for the work He has planned for you. The entire body becomes involved in serving as a vessel, a tool, a worker for Christ not because you have to, but because you want to. You, in fact, become one of God's tools, a living part of the action, involved in sharing what you have with others. In your bodily form others see that you either belong to God or you do not. The choice is up to each individual and the choice is made freely.

- "A living and holy sacrifice, acceptable to God"—The person we present to God must begin to abide in God. 1 Peter 2:1–3 (NAS) tells us this, "Therefore, putting aside all malice, and all guile, and hypocrisy, and envy, and all slander, like newborn babes, long for the pure milk of the word, that by it you may grow in respect to salvation, if you have tasted the kindness of the Lord."

What more need be said? There are certain things we need to rid our lives of which are not good in their present form. For some of us, lusts of the body will have to be dealt with. Others may have to rid themselves of some fleshly deeds and acts which are unhealthy, knowing that the flesh has been corrupted by wrongfulness. All of us are capable of sinning in the flesh as quickly as we sin in the mind. Sinfulness in any form must be tended to promptly, as it is unacceptable to God. We must rid ourselves of that self-seeking nature that seeks to satisfy itself by the things we know are wrong and draws us away from God.

A living and holy sacrifice does not mean you withdraw from the world, but rather that you set yourself aside from the worldly (carnal) standards. You will begin to seek godliness in your life and separate yourself from willful sin. A living sacrifice says, "No, I will not willingly partake of wrongful deeds and sinfulness." Honestly, that's not too much of a sacrifice for us to make, when you think about it, because we don't need sin in our lives anyway. Godliness is a much more acceptable way of life and leads to happiness. We can only learn through our efforts to live like Christ.

- "Do not be conformed to this world"—And just why not! Because the committed life, the transformed life, the abundant life is not found in the misleading systems of worldliness. Worldliness says, "Get it now! Get it for yourself at any cost!" When we live by the standard "me first," then we are conforming to the worldly standards. The world does not seek after God, but leans toward self-satisfaction and "what's in it for me." As Christians we don't need to live with that kind of attitude.

  Christian, don't be fooled into believing you can walk on the edge, living in the Spirit and still having the things that fulfill the desires of the carnal heart. You can't! The time has come to make a decision. By presenting your life to Christ you have to quit believing you can give Christ just a tiny part of your life to work with and thinking you will gain the abundant life in that manner.

It doesn't work that way. To be a fulfilled Christian you have to submit to Christ as authority over your life. We must rid ourselves of things which lead us away from God. Honestly, it isn't all that hard to do. And with your commitment of faith and trust, it grows easier step by step because Christ leads the way.

We must not be conformed to this world's carnal standards because we will be led into all sorts of problems that have no solution. The carnal world does not live in God's light but seeks to hide in spiritual darkness and the shadow of evil. I hope you understand the only way to lasting happiness is to rid yourself of the carnal life and seek new insight concerning the Spirit of God.

- "Be transformed by the renewing of a mind, that you may prove what the will of God is"—The renewing of the mind produces goodness and godliness in life. The "old spirit" is dulled by the carnal nature, but godliness brings a sparkle to life that is unobtainable anywhere except through God. Even if the "old spirit" (the carnal nature) has all a person could want materially, something will still be missing—Christ.

The renewed mind grasps the importance of making promises and following through with them. The renewed mind becomes steadfast and stabilized while the "old spirit" wavers and falters by every problem that arises because the renewed spirit clings to the promises and Word of God.

The transformed spirit seeks the truth and finds it. The "old spirit" is shielded from the truths of God. No wonder commitment to Christ is desirable; our spirits become alive with the spirit of the living Lord, and He gives us the abiding life that all Christians are meant to experience.

BE ANCHORED

"Therefore, my beloved brethren, be steadfast, immovable, always abounding in the work of the Lord, knowing that your toil is not in vain in the Lord." 1 Corinthians 15:58 (NAS) When we are tossed around by the storms of life what do we have to hang on to for hope and security? Who will save us from destruction? Where is our hope? All of the answers are the same, Christ Jesus our Lord and Savior.

Christians, committed or not, have this firm hope, this security, as we discover that Christ is our anchor throughout life. He alone can calm the storms of life. Do you recall the story of Jesus calming the storm in Luke 8:22–25? If you aren't sure of all of the facts, read it again and refresh your spirit. Jesus merely rebuked the storm and the surging waves fell silent. The storm was calmed. The power of the Almighty God was at work to ease a very troubled situation. Jesus put the storm to rest then, and He still does today. That's the way Jesus is—always confident and with full authority no matter what may come.

Be anchored in Christ, for nothing tosses Him around. Even Satan could not have his way with Christ. You had best believe that if Satan could overcome our Lord he would have but *he could not!* Christ is our anchor, our stronghold on life both now and throughout eternity. He is unmovable and secure. As we commit our lives to Christ to follow Him and be His person then we too will be firmly anchored in faith and trust.

COMMIT YOUR WAYS
TO LEARNING THE TRUTH

What truth? God's is, of course, the real truth. The truth that matters, that makes a difference. You see, the worldly system does not know God's truth. The world is misled by a series of lies. The carnal system teaches that we can live quite well without God. God's truth as seen in the Bible is that we cannot live a complete and happy life without Him. Apart from God we are nothing, but in God, and through God, we are everything.

Let me probe the truths of God a little deeper with you. God sent His Son into this world to change the world to lead us back to fellowship with Him, and provide us with a new life in Jesus. When Jesus left this earth, He sent the Holy Spirit to take His place, as our Helper, Comforter, and as our personal Guide to lead us into the fullness of the Christian life. The Holy Spirit guides us to God through our efforts to read the Bible, study it, ponder it, and believe it. The Bible reenforces our beliefs, and we should be sensitive to the Spirit as He teaches us.

The truths of God reveal the lies of Satan to us. It is by seeking the truth that we learn to walk in the Spirit. For without the truth of God in our lives we are empty shells. My life, without God, is worthless and nothing. But with the truth of God implanted in my heart I am a productive child of the living God. Only by discovering the truth and exercising our privilege of reading our Bibles can we become a well-informed people. You see, unless God works through us and in us, very little of the truth ever shines forth. We are his vessels of sharing the truth and because of our commitment the truth goes out to those who will listen and wait to learn the promises of God.

COMMITMENT MEANS TOTAL AND COMPLETE LOVE TO CHRIST

How much do you really love Christ the Lord? Do you love Him all the time or part-time? The truth is many of us are "part-time Christians." Part-time Christians are happy to worship on Sunday morning. After they leave the services they seldom consider Christ at all. Then when the next Sunday rolls around they're back in the same old pews playing the role of part-time Christian. The part-timer seldom sees much of anything spiritual occurring in their lives. They sit back and wonder why life is passing them by, and they aren't experiencing the same joy they see in other Christians.

Our promises of commitment should lead us toward a full commitment of faith. Everything we do as Christians should point back to our commitment of faith and trust. As we follow Christ and maintain our commitment, He fulfills our promises and allows our faith to grow.

To live the life filled with promise we have to learn: Jesus Christ first, others are second, and yourself last

With our commitment to love we begin to experience an overflowing of love in our spiritual fountain. We can never give away more love than we receive as we follow the course of JOY— Jesus, Others and Yourself. The Spirit fills us over and over as our love flows and fills the hearts of others. The love we gain, *agape* love (unselfish, God-type love) gives without expectation of anything in return. It is a love that strives to be usable and be shared.

You cannot live a life of promise and hope without love. Christ considered it all important and said, "There is no greater love than this; to lay down your life for a friend." That is exactly what Christ did for you and me in giving complete love for us to abide in. We can now share that same love with others.

COMMITMENT—OPENNESS

The life filled with promise and hope is respected by all. It is a life that is viewed by others. As others see our lives as vessels, instruments of God, then they will want the same qualities in their lives.

I used to be concerned that people would take advantage of me, as a Christian writer, because I open my life to you, my readers. I was fearful that people would say unkind things and treat me with indifference as I shared how Christ is working in my life. Actually nothing of the sort has happened. Quite the reverse has occurred. One person approached me yesterday and said, "I don't know how you can open your life like you do but I'm sure glad you do. I have learned so much about myself and my life in Christ from reading your *Book of Devotions for Today's Woman*. And to think I almost didn't pick it up and read it because I am a man and I thought your book was just for women. I wish all the men I know would read it. So much of your life displays the normal Christian life and our experiences. Your devotional book reflected many of the same struggles I have had. The solutions you found re-enforced what the Lord has taught me in the same circumstances."

We need not be overly fearful of being open and vulnerable. What the negative forces we encounter think about us really isn't all that important, and we soon learn that everything that happens can carry us toward a more in depth relationship with Christ. And that, after all, is one of our major goals as maturing Christians.

Open Lives Hide No Secrets!   A life that is pleasing to the Lord is achieved as we open the doors of our spiritual hearts and allow His perfect love to flow through us.

HE LIVETH IN ME

Commitment to Christ, agreeing in promise, action, and deed that we promise to make Jesus Lord of our lives, means that we allow Him to live in and through us. Knowing the will of God is not always easy, but we can be certain of this—Christ alone reveals the blessings of the abundant life.

When He lives in us we are pleased and glad to be ourselves. I don't have to try to be like you and you surely don't have to strive to be like me. We are individuals, created differently, exclusively, to be a certain person. I cannot fit into your pattern of life nor can you fit into mine. God doesn't want us to. He wants us to run our individual races, not in competition with each other, but lending full support to one another.

Paul's words seem to say, "I have run *my race,* I have finished *my course,* I have done the things *I made a commitment to do.*" We run the race, Paul teaches, not to win each other's prize but to gain our own prize and reward from God. Surely, God wouldn't want me to have the prize intended for you. He wants me to run my race and claim my special trophy.

Unless we allow Christ to function through us, as Christians, we will miss God's plan for our lives. We can search anywhere and everywhere for the untouchable blessings of the abiding life but never lay hold of them unless Christ is living in us. Now truly, when we consider it, do any of us want to leave our prize to go unclaimed? I think not!

COMMITMENT— OBEDIENCE TO GOD

There is no way to make a commitment to God without being obedient. With our promise to be God's total person, we must decide to obey His standards. We will cast aside unbelief, and desire to be obedient children so that we can have full fellowship with the Father.

Obedience takes determination. By knowing God's way is better than our way, then we will learn to obey Him. We must follow Christ's example and obey the will of God in our daily lives. Without doing so, we cannot fully experience the abiding life.

COMMITMENT—
TO GROW AND MATURE

All the promises we make, all the answered prayers and joys we experience are fulfilled through the power of God. With our commitment of trust and faith the Lord graciously allows us to grow and mature in faith.

The maturing Christian finds that the mind set on Christ is not searching and seeking needlessly and in vain. It has found that Christ is our all. Through Him we find all our needs. For the maturing Christian there is a responsibility to walk with Him twenty-four hours at a time, day in, day out. We need nothing outside of Him and we must seek full understanding of Him. Our maturing faith demonstrates His perfect love as it flows through us.

There is more to Christian commitment than meets the eye. While not all Christians commit their entire lives to Christ, all are aware that there is a need to be all that Christ wants us to be. It is only as we face the reality that we have failed in making a personal promise to the Lord that we can begin to solve the problem of lack of commitment. We need to live above our circumstances and our problems, and the only way to do that is through a complete commitment to Christ. He waits to take our burdens and tend our needs. He does not force commitment on us, but when we promise to be fully His, then He opens new doors of faith and understanding to us.

We shirk commitment because we fear God will make us do or be something we want no part of, but the truth is with full commitment to Christ we can reach and strive for our goal—to be more Christ-like everyday.

Questions

1. What does commitment mean to you?
2. How can you present your life to Christ?

3. How should a commitment or promise to Christ be made?

4. Why is a submissive spirit necessary to achieve full commitment to Christ?

5. Why is it necessary to renew your mind through your personal commitment to the Lord?

6. What kind of sacrifices do you think Christ intends you to make with your promises to follow Him?

7. Why should the Christian not conform to the standards of the self-seeking world we live in?

8. How are Christians to live a life that is different and varied from that of the nonbeliever?

9. Who anchors us in our faith?

10. How can Christ possibly calm the worst situations we encounter?

11. What can we learn as we read, study, and ponder the Scriptures?

12. Why is it vital that we expand our knowledge and understanding of the Bible?

13. Why, do you think, has God given us the Bible as a book of truth, wisdom, and knowledge?

14. How important is openness in the Christian life? Why?

15. Why must we obey God?

16. What happens when we deliberately disobey God?

10

Promises to cherish

We need to take one last look at some important promises mentioned in the Bible. Not necessarily to examine them but to better understand them. Our study of commitment has led us into some of the deeper things of God. None of us wants to turn away, at this point, and not make some important promises to God. But what are some of the things we need to ponder as we consider our own personal promises to our Lord. Read along with me and allow our Lord to lead you in the right direction concerning promises and commitment.

- James 1:2, 3 (Williams) "You must consider it the purest joy, my brothers, when you are involved in various trials, for you surely know that what is genuine in your faith produces the patient mind that endures."

Thought. My trials are known by the Lord. He has promised that through these trials my faith will be refined and purified. He has promised that no matter how distant and far away I feel He is, He is still with me. He has not abandoned me but has provided His Spirit to guide me through the storms of life. And with the patience learned through my ordeal my faith grows firmer and stronger.

- Acts 2:38b, 39 (Williams) "You must repent and, as an expression of it, let every one of you be baptized in the name of Jesus Christ—that you may have your sins forgiven; and then you will receive the gift of the Holy Spirit, for the promise belongs to you and your children, as well as to all those who are far away whom the Lord our God may call to Him."

Thought. What a promise! Allow the Lord to speak to your heart that you may have full understanding and knowledge of these two verses.

- 2 Corinthians 12:9b (NKJV) "My grace is sufficient for you, for My strength is made perfect in weaknesses."

Thought. The Lord clearly states it and therefore we may believe that His grace is all sufficient for us. He is all we need. When we are at our weakest, then His strength and power will see us through. His power is perfect and complete. What more encouragement should we need from the Savior? He has used the word "sufficient" so that we might understand the completeness and fullness of His authority. Talk about commitment, His commitment to us is perfect strength and power through a full knowledge that He has provided us with His spirit to live within us. *Wow!*

- 2 Corinthians 5:17 (NKJV) "If anyone is in Christ, he is a new creation; old things have passed away; behold, all things have become new."

Thought. Look at this, Christian friend, "anyone" in Christ has become a new creation, remade, reborn. The old things and habits have passed away because Christ is ours. We don't have to remain in the old state in sinfulness and hopelessness, Christ has given us new life, new hope. Talk about *special promises* consider this one and claim it for your own.

- Isaiah 1:18 (NAS) "Come now, and let us reason together, says the Lord, though your sins are as scarlet, they will be as white as snow; though they are red like crimson, they will be like wool."

Thought.   Our Lord, the Almighty and gracious Lord, says for us to reason together. How wonderful! His promises are that our sins will be washed as white as snow and will be like wool. Consider how good our Lord is that He keeps His promises. When He speaks, it is done.

Don't overlook the fact that the Lord has told you to reason this thing through. Ponder this thought. God is speaking to your heart and to mine. What can we do to earn this forgiveness? Why are we so special that God is willing to forgive and forget? It's all because of Jesus. We, as followers of Christ, have been washed clean and given a new beginning. Jesus did it all, and only because we accept His gracious gift are we worthy of anything.

- 2 Timothy 1:8, 9 (NAS) "Do not be ashamed of the testimony of our Lord, or of me His prisoner; but join with me in suffering for the gospel according to the power of God, who has saved us, and called us with a holy calling, not according to our works, but according to His own purpose and grace which was granted us in Christ Jesus from all eternity."

Thought.   These words should encourage your spirit. It is my hope that you receive a full understanding of them as you meditate on them day and night.

- 2 Timothy 2:12–14 (NAS) "For I know whom I have believed and I am convinced that He is able to guard what I have entrusted to Him until that day, Retain the standard of sound words which you have heard from me, in the faith and love which are in Christ Jesus. Guard, through the Holy Spirit who dwells in you, the treasure which has been entrusted to you."

Thought.   There is a great deal of information to consider in these two verses:

1. Paul tells us that he is convinced that Christ is able to guard what he has entrusted to Him until that day. Paul seems to say, "Jesus can take care of whatever I hand over to Him, anytime, anywhere not only for now, but for time eternal. Jesus keeps His words." The Lord's promises and trust are secure and we are secure in Christ because Christ is our Lord.

2. By retaining sound words, words from the Scriptures, teachings of God, you will be safe and secure. Don't stray away to unproven doctrine and unsafe techniques which show you a better way. Christ is the way, the truth, and the life.

3. The Holy Spirit is the watchdog of our faith. He tends to us and allows us to see those who seek to mislead us. The Holy Spirit guards our treasure, our prize, which is ours through a life that is committed to trusting and knowing the Lord.

Our viewing of Scripture could go on and on and with each promise we will grow in faith. Since my space is limited, allow me to provide you with a list of verses which will encourage your heart and anchor your faith deeper in the Lord Jesus Christ. The Scriptures will be given you at the end of this chapter.

Whatever promises you and I make should be viewed as vows of faith. When we vow to serve the Lord we must be sincere in our desires to be His person. We must be willing to obey and not turn aside when the storm clouds roll in. We must believe, trust, and step forward in faith knowing that whatever comes our way, regardless of the results, our Lord stands firm. We are secure in Him because He has given us His full attention. He has said His grace is sufficient and we must accept this fact.

One of the greatest challenges a Christian can encounter is making a full commitment of faith to Christ. Perhaps you are at that point right this moment. You have reviewed the information in this book and you know beyond any doubt the time is right and you need to follow the Lord to the best of your abilities, totally and completely. If that is the need you have at this moment please consider my prayer for you.

Dear Lord,

I am ready to give you my all. I've been holding out on you Lord because I wasn't sure I could make a full commitment to you but now I know, I know with no doubt, that I must have the abiding life, the abundant life you have set aside for me.

Lord consider me worthy enough to press me into service. Allow your love to flow through me so that others may know my commitment to life is based in you. I am willing, Lord, and ready, to give each area of my life over to you. I believe Lord that you will improve my life and my character and allow me to share my personal witness with others throughout my life.

Lord, keep me strong, be my stronghold in the storms of life. Allow me the understanding and wisdom which you seek each child of God to have, so that I might fully understand the person you want me to be. Teach my spirit the things I must know and open my spiritual eyes and ears that I might receive the mysteries of the faith fully.

Thank you Lord for your gift of salvation, for the forgiveness of sins and for providing me with a better way of life. I believe in you, I trust you, and I accept whatever you give me with a spirit of anticipation and love. Allow my spirit to understand, as it has never understood before, the necessity for a commitment to you in my life. I love you Lord and give praise and thanks to your name. Amen.

It would make me very happy to know of your personal commitments to Christ through your understanding of *Promises*. Please take a few moments to write me a note. It would bless my life and lift my spirit. God bless you for your decisions and your consideration of promises made and promises kept. Press on, servant of the living Lord.

Write me!

Scriptures of Encouragement

Philippians 4:19

John 14:27

Colossians 2:6

Isaiah 30:18

Psalms 19:7, 8

John 12:26

Malachi 3:7

Hebrews 5:9

Proverbs 11:18

Psalms 34:10

Psalms 3:5

Romans 8:32

John 6:37

Exodus 19:5

1 John 2:17

Psalms 119:2

1 Peter 5:6

Psalms 37:18

Index

Acts of the Apostles, 20, 116, 144
Affirmation of trust, 65
Amon, 120
Apollos, 126
Aquila, 126

Barnabas, 116–19
Bearing fruit, 115–27
Belief, 59–60
  (*See also* Commitment)
*Book of Devotions for Today's
  Woman, A* (Carroll), 31, 105, 139
Buckelew, Roy, 117–18

Career, 24
Carnal nature, 90, 91, 134
Change, areas in need of, 67–68
Children, 2
Christ-centered people, 40–44
  qualities of, 44–47
Christian maturity, 68–69, 72–75,
  106
Colossians, 16, 91–92, 148
Commitment, 14, 16, 19–33
  bearing fruit, 115–27

challenge of, 37–40
defined, 131
depth of love, 109–12
to family, 24–25
God's people of, 57–75
to grow in faith, 89–100
ideas, 23–24
to job and career, 24
lack of, 52–54
to parents, 25–27
personal, 28–30
personal call to, 60–62, 64
to pray, 32
projects, 23
purpose of, 35–37
sharing faith, 30–31
steps toward, 129–42
Confidence, 106
1 Corinthians, 14, 15, 47, 64, 70,
  71, 106, 135
2 Corinthians, 73, 144

Darkness, 10–13
Desirable qualities of life, 35–55
Discipline, 37

Doubts, 79–80
    patterns of, 77–78

Ecclesiastes, 49
Ephesians, 11, 16, 58, 73, 78–79, 93
Exodus, 148

Faith, 19, 20
    commitment to grow in, 89–100
    sharing, 30–31
Family, commitment to, 24–25
Fears, 80–85
Freedom through Christ, allowing
    yourself, 62–65
Friendships, 102

Galatians, 65, 79, 97
Gideon, 122–23
Giving, 73–74
God's people of commitment, 57–75

Hebrews, 21, 72–73, 122, 148
Helkiah, 121
Holy Spirit, 7, 8–9, 14, 48, 62, 67,
    78, 116, 117, 137, 146
*How to Talk with Your Children
    About God* (Carroll), 2

Ideas, 23–24
Immature Christians, 69–72
Isaiah, 145, 148

James, 11–12, 49, 143
Jesus Christ:
    baptism of, 4
    commitment of, 35–37
    light of, 10–13
    ministry of, 4–6
Job, 24
John, 4–6, 11, 20, 46, 148
1 John, 21, 79, 108–10, 148
John the Baptist, 4, 124
Joseph of Arimathea, 124–25
Josiah, 120–22
Judges, 122

2 Kings, 120–22
Knowledge, 48, 66

Legalism, 58
Light, 10–13
Limited Christian lifestyle, 51
Love, 46–48, 101–13, 137–38
Luke, 4, 6, 49, 123–24, 136

Malachi, 148
Mannasseh, 120
Mark, 4, 6
Mary, 27
Matthew, 4, 6

Negativeness, 62, 83–85
Nicodemus, 5
Nominal Christian lifestyle, 51, 52–
    54

Obedience, 140
Older people, 25–27
Openness, 138–39

Parents, commitment to, 25–27
Part-time Christians, 137–38
Paul, 13–16, 70, 71, 92, 96–97, 107,
    116–17, 123, 133, 140, 146
Personal commitments, 28–30
1 Peter, 48, 85, 86, 133, 148
Pharisees, 11
Philippians, 16, 95, 97, 107, 148
Pilate, 125
Pleasing God, 83–87
Prayer, 32, 147
Pretending, 83
Priscilla, 126
Projects, 23
Promises, 28–29, 31, 143–48
    (*See also* Commitment)
Proverbs, 49, 148
Provisions, 98
Psalms, 11, 21, 84, 85, 148

Rejection, 101–3

Revelation, 12
Romans, 64, 79, 92–93, 95–96, 133,
    148

Salvation (eternal life), 1, 2
Satan, 12, 136, 137
Self, 96–97
Selflessness, 95–96, 108
Shaphran, 121
Spiritual growth, stages of, 70–72
Spiritual immaturity, 70–72
Spiritual maturity, 68–69, 72–75,
    106
Stephen, 116
Striking remarks, 50

Submissivesness, 132–35

Teachableness, 66–68
Thessalonians, 16
1 Timothy, 16
2 Timothy, 16, 145–46
Total Christian lifestyle, 51–52
Trusting, 65, 83
Truth, 136–37

Vulnerability, 101, 102, 105

Wisdom, 48–49
Wordly opinions, 50–51